PR5860
Robins
Radica.

W9-DAM-551

DATE DUE

JAN 2 7 1988			

HIGHSMITH 45-220

Radical Literary Education

Jeffrey C. Robinson

Radical Literary Education

A Classroom Experiment with Wordsworth's "Ode"

887-213

The University of Wisconsin Press

Published 1987

The University of Wisconsin Press
114 North Murray Street
Madison, Wisconsin 53715

The University of Wisconsin Press, Ltd.
1 Gower Street
London WC1E 6HA, England

Copyright © 1987
The Board of Regents of the University of Wisconsin System
All rights reserved

First printing

Printed in the United States of America

For LC CIP information see the colophon

ISBN 0-299-11060-5 cloth; 0-299-11064-8 paper

To Jeanie
"Companion never lost through many a league"

. . . those obstinate questionings
Of sense and outward things,
Fallings from us, vanishings;
Blank misgivings of a Creature
Moving about in worlds not realised,
High instincts before which our mortal Nature
Did tremble like a guilty Thing surprised:

William Wordsworth

I do not regard the general ability to read and write as progress.

Siegfried Bernfeld

Contents

Acknowledgments

Reporting in some detail on students specifically as readers in their adolescence, I have had to separate myself from that stage of life and that readership. The new stage of uncertainty, called middle life, nonetheless allows me the freedom to acknowledge my gratitude to the students in English 200 at the University of Colorado, Boulder, 1982–85.

I would also like to thank Professor Lesley Brill, former chair of the Department of English, for encouraging an atmosphere congenial to pedagogical experimentation. Professors Martin Bickman, Bruce Kawin, and James R. Kincaid have generously read part or all of the manuscript and offered informed suggestions, as did Professor Peter J. Manning of the University of Southern California. A conversation with Dr. Henry P. Coppolillo, a child psychiatrist at the University of Colorado Health Sciences Center, stimulated an important line of thinking for this study. A reviewer for the University of Wisconsin Press, Professor Kenneth Johnston of Indiana University, also commented thoughtfully and extensively on my work. My father, Dr. Arthur Robinson, read the manuscript with care and offered valuable stylistic suggestions. The Press's sympathetic director, Allen Fitchen, has given enthusiastic support.

Thanks, too, go to typists Carolyn Dameron, Colleen Anderson, and Marje Urban.

xii Acknowledgments

The reader of this book will encounter repeatedly the voices of two critics and teachers essential to the past-and-ongoing dialogue with myself about literature and education: Professor Allen Grossman of Brandeis University and the late Lionel Trilling.

Denver
December 1985

Ode: Intimations of Immortality from Recollections of Early Childhood

The Child is father of the Man;
And I could wish my days to be
Bound each to each by natural piety.

I

There was a time when meadow, grove, and stream,
The earth, and every common sight,
To me did seem
Apparelled in celestial light,
The glory and the freshness of a dream.
It is not now as it hath been of yore;—
Turn wheresoe'er I may,
By night or day,
The things which I have seen I now can see no more.

II

The Rainbow comes and goes,
And lovely is the Rose,
The Moon doth with delight
Look round her when the heavens are bare;
Waters on a starry night
Are beautiful and fair;
The sunshine is a glorious birth;
But yet I know, where'er I go,
That there hath past away a glory from the earth.

III

Now, while the birds thus sing a joyous song,
  And while the young lambs bound
    As to the tabor's sound,
To me alone there came a thought of grief:
A timely utterance gave that thought relief,
    And I again am strong:
The cataracts blow their trumpets from the steep;
No more shall grief of mine the season wrong;
I hear the Echoes through the mountains throng,
The Winds come to me from the fields of sleep,
    And all the earth is gay;
      Land and sea
   Give themselves up to jollity,
    And with the heart of May
   Doth every Beast keep holiday; —
    Thou Child of Joy,
Shout round me, let me hear thy shouts, thou happy Shepherd-
  boy!

IV

Ye blessèd Creatures, I have heard the call
  Ye to each other make; I see
The heavens laugh with you in your jubilee;
  My heart is at your festival,
    My head hath its coronal,
The fulness of your bliss, I feel — I feel it all.
    Oh evil day! if I were sullen
    While Earth herself is adorning,
     This sweet May-morning,
    And the Children are culling
     On every side,
   In a thousand valleys far and wide,
    Fresh flowers; while the sun shines warm,
And the Babe leaps up on his Mother's arm: —
    I hear, I hear, with joy I hear!

— But there's a Tree, of many, one,
A single Field which I have looked upon,
Both of them speak of something that is gone:
         The Pansy at my feet
         Doth the same tale repeat:
Whither is fled the visionary gleam?
Where is it now, the glory and the dream?

V

Our birth is but a sleep and a forgetting:
The Soul that rises with us, our life's Star,
         Hath had elsewhere its setting,
            And cometh from afar:
         Not in entire forgetfulness,
         And not in utter nakedness,
But trailing clouds of glory do we come
         From God, who is our home:
Heaven lies about us in our infancy!
Shades of the prison-house begin to close
         Upon the growing Boy,
            But He
Beholds the light, and whence it flows,
         He sees it in his joy;
The Youth, who daily farther from the east
         Must travel, still is Nature's Priest,
         And by the vision splendid
         Is on his way attended;
At length the Man perceives it die away,
And fade into the light of common day.

VI

Earth fills her lap with pleasures of her own;
Yearnings she hath in her own natural kind,
And, even with something of a Mother's mind,
         And no unworthy aim,
         The homely Nurse doth all she can

To make her Foster-child, her Inmate Man,
      Forget the glories he hath known,
And that imperial palace whence he came.

VII

Behold the Child among his new-born blisses,
A six years' Darling of a pigmy size!
See, where 'mid work of his own hand he lies,
Frettied by sallies of his mothers's kisses,
With light upon him from his father's eyes!
See, at his feet, some little plan or chart,
Some fragment from his dream of human life,
Shaped by himself with newly-learned art;
      A wedding or a festival,
      A mourning or a funeral;
        And this hath now his heart,
      And unto this he frames his song:
        Then will he fit his tongue
To dialogues of business, love, or strife;
      But it will not be long
      Ere this be thrown aside,
      And with new joy and pride
The little Actor cons another part;
Filling from time to time his "humorous stage"
With all the Persons, down to palsied Age,
That Life brings with her in her equipage;
      As if his whole vocation
      Were endless imitation.

VIII

Thou, whose exterior semblance doth belie
      Thy Soul's immensity;
Thou best Philosopher, who yet dost keep
Thy heritage, thou Eye among the blind,
That, deaf and silent, read'st the eternal deep,
Haunted for ever by the eternal mind, —

Mighty Prophet! Seer blest!
On whom those truths do rest,
Which we are toiling all our lives to find,
In darkness lost, the darkness of the grave;
Thou, over whom thy Immortality
Broods like the Day, a Master o'er a Slave,
A Presence which is not to be put by;
Thou little Child, yet glorious in the might
Of heaven-born freedom on thy being's height,
Why with such earnest pains dost thou provoke
The years to bring the inevitable yoke,
Thus blindly with thy blessedness at strife?
Full soon thy Soul shall have her earthly freight,
And custom lie upon thee with a weight,
Heavy as frost, and deep almost as life!

IX

O joy! that in our embers
Is something that doth live,
That nature yet remembers
What was so fugitive!
The thought of our past years in me doth breed
Perpetual benediction: not indeed
For that which is most worthy to be blest;
Delight and liberty, the simple creed
Of Childhood, whether busy or at rest,
With new-fledged hope still fluttering in his breast: —
Not for these I raise
The song of thanks and praise;
But for those obstinate questionings
Of sense and outward things,
Fallings from us, vanishings;
Blank misgivings of a Creature
Moving about in worlds not realised,
High instincts before which our mortal Nature
Did tremble like a guilty Thing surprised:

But for those first affections,
Those shadowy recollections,
Which, be they what they may,
Are yet the fountain light of all our day,
Are yet a master light of all our seeing;
Uphold us, cherish, and have power to make
Our noisy years seem moments in the being
Of the eternal Silence: truths that wake,
To perish never;
Which neither listlessness, nor mad endeavour,
Nor Man nor Boy,
Nor all that is at enmity with joy,
Can utterly abolish or destroy!
Hence in a season of calm weather
Though inland far we be,
Our Souls have sight of that immortal sea
Which brought us hither,
Can in a moment travel thither,
And see the Children sport upon the shore,
And hear the mighty waters rolling evermore.

X

Then sing, ye Birds, sing, sing a joyous song!
And let the young Lambs bound
As to the tabor's sound!
We in thought will join your throng,
Ye that pipe and ye that play,
Ye that through your hearts to-day
Feel the gladness of the May!
What though the radiance which was once so bright
Be now for ever taken from my sight,
Though nothing can bring back the hour
Of splendour in the grass, of glory in the flower;
We will grieve not, rather find
Strength in what remains behind;
In the primal sympathy

Which having been must ever be;
In the soothing thoughts that spring
Out of human suffering;
In the faith that looks through death,
In years that bring the philosophic mind.

XI

And O, ye Fountains, Meadows, Hills, and Groves,
Forebode not any severing of our loves!
Yet in my heart of hearts I feel your might;
I only have relinquished one delight
To live beneath your more habitual sway.
I love the Brooks which down their channels fret,
Even more than when I tripped lightly as they;
The innocent brightness of a new-born Day
       Is lovely yet;
The Clouds that gather round the setting sun
Do take a sober colouring from an eye
That hath kept watch o'er man's mortality;
Another race hath been, and other palms are won.
Thanks to the human heart by which we live,
Thanks to its tenderness, its joys, and fears,
To me the meanest flower that blows can give
Thoughts that do often lie too deep for tears.

Part One
Introduction

1   A Problem in Literary Education

The following case study of an introductory literature class eluci-
dates what I see to be a contemporary deficiency in literature
instruction and offers one possible solution. Simply put, students
need to develop and exercise an historical imagination in the
presence of literature; this, in the English and American tradition of literary education, they seldom do. In order to discover
a work of literature as an event both making and made by various histories and contexts readers must discover themselves in
something like a comparable history. That is, such work encourages the critical self-consciousness of a political person, which,
for the late-adolescent student, should come naturally. The course
which I have developed and which I here comment upon used
as its occasion Wordsworth's "Ode: Intimations of Immortality
from Recollections of Early Childhood."[1] To represent this experience of literary education as faithfully as I can, I will offer
three subjects in detail: the student and the teacher (working and
learning together) and the poem. Necessarily much of this study
is about the "Ode" recovered in its own contexts.

The course I am about to describe came toward the end of
about two decades of labor in the profession of English Studies,

1. William Wordsworth, *Poetical Works,* ed. Ernest de Selincourt and Helen
Darbishire (Oxford: Clarendon, 1958), 4:279–85. See pp. xiii–xix.

mostly at the University of Colorado at Boulder. By the usual standards of judgment I would have to be considered a successful teacher, but—particularly in this second decade—I became discontent with the matter and methods and purposes of English Studies and was forced to reevaluate my work, often to the point of wishing to abandon what has at times seemed a worse than useless activity. Raised in a family that has valued and in fact worshipped the arts as a phenomenon transcendent of contemporary life and society and transcendent of dialogue and argument, a phenomenon confirming a final vision, through art, of an idyllic if mysterious harmony, I entered my profession buoyed by the assumption that the teacher of literature ought to transmit this same vision to his students. That the study of literature ought to be "disinterested," or apolitical, also was an assumption that needed no challenge: I was a fervent New Critic, cemented in my position by a Harvard education that deepened my "love" for literature through the pervasive values of Christian humanism that sacralized the great books for me before I had ever opened them. It has only been through a growing impatience with the increasingly reactionary politics of the last fifteen years, through the example of feminism, and through a personal analysis which helped me see the private reasons for clinging to literature-as-consolation that I have begun to consider how the mind, acting in the midst of and through a sense of social commitments, can further engage the issues of its own and previous civilizations.

Theodor Adorno's comment that "life has become appearance" is nowhere more dramatically obvious than in the college literature classroom, where young people and their teacher talk about losses and restoration, grief and desire, revolutions and tyrannies, form and content, in ways that satisfy the hunger for order and coherence and the chaste idyll of beauty. Yet this particular satisfaction rarely bridges the gap between the pastoral play inside the classroom and the life outside of it. Indeed, it only further divides the student from his or her sense of the present and future. Today the effect of this gap seems, ironically, to support the student's fantasies about security: if I make enough money or marry into wealth, I can acquire for myself a version of the idyll of literary experience. This, of course, is a version of the claim that capitalism has always made — that happiness can be bought. But living in a world in which, as Allen Grossman has said, to our minds the nuclear bomb has already dropped, this becomes capitalism *in extremis*.

Examples of, in Lifton's phrase, "psychic numbing" abound in the classroom. How rare is it for a student, much less a class of students, to grow uneasy about what really is the anachronism of many of the great books in the nuclear age? Consider the formulation of the "underworld" or the world of the shades in Homer, Virgil, and Dante (a place that confers meaning and moral judgment upon the living members of that civilization) and the "convention" of the living hero reaching out across time for contact with one of those shades (Achilles to Patroclus, Aeneas to Dido) only to discover himself tragically bound to his own longing. For the reader, that longing and the tragedy are made thoroughly palatable by the assumption that meaning and trust in the process of human life are assured by the fact of generations. Yet students now are growing up with the knowledge that generations may come to an end; even this possibility rends asunder their trust in generations and ought, logically, to make them look at the *Iliad* and their thoughts and feelings about the *Iliad* as an anachronism. That it usually does not speaks to the resilience of young people, but just as likely it can be explained by the state's wish — carried out by many of its schools and teachers and readily assimilated by students — to convince the present generation that modern life is "life as usual," just as it appears in the classics. The academic study of literature reinforces modern society's inclination to see the appearance of life as life itself, which, I will argue, is nothing less than the refusal of the historical imagination.

It seems to me that two potentially opposing educational positions have emerged: humanism and education for critical consciousness. From the traditional humanist position, the virtue of studying traditional literature is just that the great works provide a locus of simplicity and coherence and beauty; they are a relief, a consolation. As Lionel Trilling says in his beautiful report on humanist pedagogy, "Why We Read Jane Austen":

> We should never take it for granted that young people inevitably respond affirmatively to what is innovative and anti-traditional in the high artistic culture of their time; there is the distinct possibility that the students with whom I was dealing saw the contemporary novel as being of a piece with those elements of the modern dispensation which they judged to be maleficent, such as industrialism, urbanization, the multiversity. This maleficence would have to do with the reduction of their selfhood, and presumably it could be neutralized by acquaintance with the characters of Jane Austen's novels.[2]

Of Austen's work he goes on to say that there are "more trees than people": the idyllic character of these novels can stand for, from Trilling's point of view, almost any of the older works that can be viewed effectively through the wrong end of the telescope. Later in the same essay, speaking of Keats's "Ode on a Grecian Urn," he defines the urn — a paradigm of old art objects — as having "pastness as one of its attributes," pastness being another way of thinking of the idyllic function of reading. A work remains consoling when it remains distant and chaste. Or, if one contextualizes it, one tries to erect a history that supports the desire for coherence, hierarchy, simplicity.

Trilling is also saying that his students affirm the need for literature as consolation. In this I would agree although, as I shall demonstrate, they are open to something quite different. His famous 1943 story of the classroom, "Of This Time, of That Place," arranges a revealing typology of literature students. In the background of the story is the usual range of well-meaning brains to inconsequential dolts. Presumably any of the "A" students could have a crack at graduate work in English Studies. But in the foreground are what must be for Trilling the two most heroic possibilities. One can be a "genius" (Tertan), full of in-

---

2. Lionel Trilling, *The Last Decade* (New York: Harcourt Brace Jovanovich, 1979), 211–12.

sight, exuberance, sensitivity, and fully alienated from "the system" through which he can easily penetrate. But he must finally submit to the clinical categories of mental illness and abandon his education. He is, in other words, a sad, nearly tragic figure whose brilliance is totally without effect. Or one can be a public figure, a student leader (Blackburn), mean and manipulative and a cheater. He makes empty-headed readings of the works studied, yet his interpretations accord rigidly and overdeterminedly with the belief that literature is consolation. Here is the teacher, Howe, reading Blackburn's answer to a test question back to his failing student:

> "Now here: you write, 'In *The Ancient Mariner,* Coleridge lives in and transports us to a honey-sweet world where all is rich and strange, a world of charm to which we can escape from the humdrum existence of our daily lives, the world of romance. Here, in this warm and honey-sweet land of charming dreams we can relax and enjoy ourselves.' . . . many opinions are possible, but not this one. Whatever anyone believes of *The Ancient Mariner,* no one can in reason believe that it represents a — a honey-sweet world in which we can relax."
>
> "But this is what I *feel,* sir."
>
> This was well done too. Howe said, "Look Mr. Blackburn. Do you really relax with hunger and thirst, the heat and the sea-serpents, the dead men with staring eyes, Life in Death and the skeletons? Come now, Mr. Blackburn."[3]

Howe rightly fails him, but the failure in the course only seems to assure Blackburn's future, and larger, success: he simply substitutes the paradise of money for his failure at producing an acceptable paradise in interpretation; being reprimanded for his faulty reading seems, in the story's logic, to secure his place high in the economic system. The teacher is finally left bewildered because, presumably, he (or his author) can construct no enlightened categories for the student or for himself. The story ends

3. Lionel Trilling, *Of This Time, of That Place* (New York: Harcourt Brace Jovanovich, 1979), 102–3.

in the springtime, at Commencement, which turns out to be more autumnal than vernal: the faint melancholy suggests that he has learned to accept these categories and go about the business of consolation.

In 1966, teaching for the first time in my life, I had a vision of the plight of students and their teachers which Trilling's story brings to mind. A journal entry I wrote describing it now helps me to understand the melancholy solution to "Of This Time, of That Place":

> Today I was chatting with the Dean of Freshmen about various students and their personal problems. I mentioned one boy as being, in my opinion, one of the unhappiest students I had ever met. He replied that he had become surprised at *how many* students seemed to him unhappy. "Perhaps it is just part of getting an education," he said. After we had finished talking, I thought of this boy, then of all these students, and then of the faculty. A sad, yet slightly humorous image rose before me — first of the faculty, as giants, as titans ranging far and wide over the race of the earth, feet on the ground, eyes lighting on the heavens, while the students were clamoring pathetically, hopelessly in the mire of their daily lives. Occasionally a giant foot would inadvertently bump a struggling mass of students.
>
> This image faded and was gradually replaced by something so touching that I could hardly sustain my vision. I saw the faculty in pain, and they were reaching down to receive succor from the students who responded and held out their hands. They met and embraced each other to assuage the pain, which kept them together forever. Together they rose into space and were swept into an orbit, like the lovers Paolo and Francesca, "swept together so lightly on the wind and still so sad."

Were I to rewrite it now, I would probably have to include both the poet and myself in the conventional academic occasion of literary study. Nor at that time did I understand the Romantic contradiction inherent in a community of alienated souls. But I got the melancholy pleasure and eerie beauty of this vision and knew that, although it was beautiful and exalted, somewhere it was wrong. What I did not know was that my vision registered the enforcement of love without desire and the insistence upon spirit without mind. Nor did I realize that what drew faculty and students into this melancholy drifting was their mutual submission to a form of oppression that distances both teacher and pupil from any form of critical thinking in the name of beauty.

Howe, sadly, does not propose the second model of education: education for critical consciousness, for which the defining term is *mind*. To stay, for a moment, with Trilling, *mind* for him became a central term — it at first was central to his early critique of the "liberal imagination" and remained so, although it underwent an important change. In the late address, "Mind in the Modern World," *mind* in its most exuberant state became a high form of *play*, in the sense that Schiller meant it, an exhibition and exercise in disinterested freedom and thus a proof of human dignity and the best fruits of a civilized society. But mind can obviously have a more "interested" function as well, one dedicated to a more critical consciousness but still full of exuberance and imagination. Again, in the Jane Austen essay, Trilling notes that Blake became for his students in the late 1960s "uniquely relevant to their spiritual aspirations" and showed a "devotion to a figure proposing impulse, excess, and the annihilation of authority" but five years later showed "devotion to the presiding genius of measure, decorum, and irony." While he accurately formulates the reception of Blake by students in the 1960s and 1970s, and thus sets up an appropriate transformation to the interest in Jane Austen, Trilling misses the real function of excess and energy in (at least the early) Blake — that energy exists to inform *mind* in a capacity which is as fully and analytically critical toward society and its artifacts as it is visionary. *Mind* for Blake is politically engaged, and so-called disinterested play of mind is a form of tyranny.

It is not, of course, fair to characterize completely Trilling's (and many others') understanding of or hope for humanism or mind-as-disinterested-play. There is not one Trilling. In the essays of *The Liberal Imagination* (1950), mind does serve critical consciousness, which in turn has been served and awakened by literature and beauty. This seems to be a hope for humanism, a hope — I fully recognize — achieved by many humanist educators. Indeed, the recent book by Carolyn Heilbrun, *Reinventing Womanhood,* includes a powerful autobiography of her experience as Trilling's student. The power comes from her tribute to him as an influence and inspiration; a tribute, however, movingly complicated by his antifeminist positions. Clearly her resistance to him did not come from his humanism, which in fact helped to stimulate critical consciousness. His willingness to think upon literature in terms of its ideas, as "great moral struggles," appealed to Heilbrun and gave her the freedom of her own ways. The problem comes as Trilling's humanism turns more and more toward the "quietism" of his 1950s and 1960s essays and more and more focused upon a disinterested play of mind. Thus "humanism," as I am using it, is not by definition custodial (of cultural artifacts) and consolatory. It only becomes so when (1) the mind's freedom joins forces with the consoling attributes of poetic beauty and (2) the critic — analyzing a poem — enforces what the Frankfurt critics Horkheimer and Adorno would consider a degraded form of Enlightenment thinking and intention: to "cast light upon" the work's dark corners by discussing its internal relations (e.g., Blackmur and Brooks) to the extent of controlling (or having the fantasy of controlling) all of the work's mystery, its otherness or subjecthood.

It may be that "humanism" retains the capacity to encompass critical thinking in the presence of the seductive idyllicism of beauty, in which case I simply experience and try to encourage my students to experience these profound tensions so defined in humanism. I wish to state my awareness that, of course, many teachers prove an exception to my view of the deficiencies in literature instruction. Not only are there plenty of good "humanist" teachers, but there is a growing number who cultivate the historical, contextualizing imagination in their literature courses, who stimulate discussion of real ideas as well as talk about the formal patterns in poetry. I would still maintain, however, that humanism in the classroom more often than not — and surely in the prominent museums of our tradition such as the Norton and Oxford anthologies — supports thinking only insofar as that thinking supports the consoling rhetoric adhering to the literary work.[4]

Trilling's older contemporary, Lewis Mumford, stated, right after the Second World War, the case for critical consciousness in American education: ". . . it is simply impossible, if we are to build up a social order advantageous to life, to keep the schools out of politics. For the school, first and last, is the modern institutional organization for interpreting social change and for converting brute compulsion and arbitrary routine into rational, enlightened, and purposive participation and control." And, more specifically, ". . . [the teacher] must not relapse into the meek pedagogue: he must become once more the Socratic gadfly, stirring up a noble discontent, not merely providing the tools for change but awakening the desire for a life in which the cash nexus and the profit motive have been exchanged for a more cooperative bond and for a more humanely amenable goal."[5] What does it mean to "stir up a noble discontent" in the classroom? A provocative answer to this question appears, by implication, in Paolo Freire's challenging *Pedagogy of the Oppressed*,[6] a directly relevant comment on education in general.

Paolo Freire has studied and evolved a theory about the education of illiterates and oppressed peoples in the Third World; for him it is a given that education is political and needs to be conducted with a full and open consciousness of this fact. The pur-

4. Similarly, the exposure to literature, sometimes with and sometimes without the help of a lively teacher, may release in the student imaginative capacities and the energy and confidence for extended rational activity. This is obvious. Yet recently a senior literature major noted to me that my course in later eighteenth-century literature — in which the literature was considered as a manifestation of Enlightenment thinking — was her first experience examining literature as an occasion for the discussion of "ideas." I think that for all the sophistication in post–New Critical theory and its efforts to join the text to other seas of thought, there is still a deeply ingrained chastity in the handling of the text itself.

5. Lewis Mumford, *Values for Survival* (New York: Harcourt, Brace and Company, 1946), 161, 163.

6. Paolo Freire, *Pedagogy of the Oppressed* (New York: Continuum, 1984).

pose of educating the oppressed in bourgeois society is to teach submission to the dominating society, to preserve an underclass position. This is comparable to Louis Althusser's argument that this purpose applies equally in bourgeois education: to teach the student submission to the ideology of the dominating class. Earlier (1927) Siegfried Bernfeld, a Freudian psychoanalyst with Marxist leanings, argued similarly that "our education is ruled by power."[7] For Freire the underclass must learn the conditions of their oppressed state and the ways in which they collaborate to preserve them. Obviously the goal is not disinterestedness but a conscious will to dissolve oppression. The teacher needs to cultivate reflection not because it is a final good but because it can produce informed and effective action. "Reflection — true reflection — leads to action."[8] Reflection, however, is not solely what we tend to think of as contemplation in solitude; rather it is a process of learning about oneself and one's environment in dialogue with a teacher who, from his or her own more conscious and enthusiastic vantage point, is learning the same things. Teachers and students, he says in a wonderful phrase, are "co-intent on reality" and eventually co-intent on its transformation, where "reality" is the particular condition of oppression. Teacher and student must not be adversaries, nor — it follows — can they simply be mutually sympathetic if that sympathy serves the conditions of domination; rather "authority must be on the side of freedom."[9] Marxists (loosely speaking) on education — such as Freire, Gramsci, Althusser, and Bernfeld — all see bourgeois education in terms of the submission to a dominant power. Proper education, on the other hand, overtly serves the cause of freedom. Both teacher and student, subject finally to the same atmosphere of oppression, must train their attention upon that reality which at basis they share.

7. See Louis Althusser's essay "Ideology and Ideological State Apparatuses," in *Lenin and Philosophy,* trans. Ben Brewster (New York: Monthly Review Press, 1971); and Siegfried Bernfeld's *Sisyphus, or the Limits of Education* (Berkeley: University of California Press, 1973).

8. Freire, *Pedagogy.*

9. Ibid.

Allowing for the abstraction of such Marxist analysis and its distance from classroom specifics, does a "pedagogy of the oppressed" apply meaningfully to the contemporary North American middle-class adolescent and his or her teacher? I think it does, to the extent that our educational system often reinforces the values of domination of one group over another, discourages historical understanding of the condition of all groups in the society, and discourages critical self-consciousness. Now, it is argued by the far Right that any form of secular humanist education encourages revolt from traditional (parental, religious) values and therefore is dangerous to the status quo. But I think that in light of our recent political history we would have to rate that danger as not very high. A more rigorous attention to critical consciousness in education is required before any kind of meaningful transformation of society in the service of freedom can occur. One can only imagine an educational community working in concert to effect such consciousness permanently in the minds of individuals and requiring repeated exposure to the notion and experience of our entanglement in oppression.

A semester-long encounter with Wordsworth's "Ode" may seem an odd way to stimulate critical consciousness. Why not read literature by women? by Blacks or Chicanos or Indians? by members of the working class?—literature, that is, by those who are or have been obviously oppressed? The value of such readings is clear. But a poem like Wordsworth's "Ode," standing squarely in the inherited tradition of the dominant class, itself voicing many of that class's privileged beliefs, possesses a reality differing from that of the literature of oppressed classes. For this is the reality of the society's educational institutions. It is also a reality inherited by teacher and student alike as an instrument, indeed a ritual, of succession and transmission. Not only does teaching the "Ode" assure that Wordsworth's major poem will be "kept alive," giving it a continuity among the generations, but it also assures the passing on of a system of values inherent in the poem, the values about and surrounding poetry, and certain values in reading and writing. The object of a "pedagogy of the oppressed" applied to Wordsworth's "Ode" is to gain a critical consciousness of this system or of, as Freire might call it, a set of "codes" which education is at pains to transmit and which we readily embrace. Literature, as the institution of our education presents it, often becomes — as I will show — an embodiment of a power structure; it retains an authority which tends to force submission to it and its values or codes. Literature in the classroom often perpetuates the association of power and domination with beauty.

In the Romantic tradition, in which modern academic literary studies are fully enmeshed, the distinguishing element of art is beauty. The experience of beauty requires the suspension of the critical faculty, the transcendence of a comprehending response to the world, the suppression of the fantasy life except for idyllic fantasies. Beauty, in this tradition, is largely defined in terms of its healing powers: it heals the psyche's wounds by providing a vision of peace and unity. Mind, in its analytical, critical capacity, acting only as a fallen instrument of ordering life in a fallen world, ceases to act in the presence of beauty and, as Keats says, ends in speculation or wonderment. The great contemporary Czech novelist, Milan Kundera, however, proposes — in *The Unbearable Lightness of Being* — an antithetical function for beauty: Tereza, a soul worn down by the tensions of the 1968 Russian invasion of Czechoslovakia, suddenly discovers "a sense of beauty" in some fortuitous occurrences with her lover, and thinks: "It was the sense of beauty that cured her of her depression and imbued her with a new will to live." For Kundera, the novelist of lives warped or stunted by absolute totalitarian government, the sense of beauty does not — as it does for Keats — "overcome all other considerations." Rather it shows the opportunity that beauty grants for the recentering of the lost soul in order to encounter with greater buoyancy the alien threats of those with power. Kundera asks whether beauty, in totalitarian states, can serve the cause of freedom and dissent. He answers that it can, if beauty engages not our desire for peace and the transcendence of social consciousness but instead a vision that the mind can be free to form its own categories when and because it is fully conscious of societal and corporate restrictions on freedom. In addition, beauty does not reinforce or encourage our narcissism or grandiosity; beauty makes us aware of limits — the limits of beauty as an extension of reality, the limits of our ability to control or shape destiny with mind itself, the limits of our power. But the reverse side of the coin of grandiosity is the sense of helplessness, the sense that totalitarian government relies on, and beauty as Kundera defines it reduces the sense of helplessness.

Jerome Bruner has imagined wonderfully what seems to me an ideal relationship between the will to action and the limits to will:

> The inverse of fate is the sense of potency — what we think is possible for us. That is to say, our view of fate shapes our sense of potency, and vice versa. Fate is the residuum that is left after one has run through the census of what is humanly possible. Each discovery of a way of proceeding, of a way of discovering, forestalling, or effecting, is, then, an incursion into fate that in effect rolls back what we take fate to be. There may one day be a beautiful formula that goes something like this: $e = p/f$, where e is the sense of human effectiveness, p is the value of all outcomes thought to be determined by human effort, and f the value of all outcomes thought to be determined by fate.[10]

The teaching of literature at present generally operates between the mutually reinforcing poles of grandiosity and helplessness, both being fantasies of human power that have at their source the single fantasy of salvation. The adolescent rescue fantasy, in psychoanalyst Peter Blos's term, focuses on a figure or object external to the self that ultimately has the power to save the individual from confusion and misery. Beauty, in the Romantic sense but not in Kundera's, serves this function. Nowhere in Bruner's formula is there any mention of a salvific power, and yet he builds into his vision the crucial role of fate. *What replaces the rescuing object is the thinking subject,* aware of its limits yet trusting in its available power.

10. Jerome Bruner, *On Knowing* (Cambridge: Harvard University Press, 1962), 159–60.

I hope that I am not simply falling into what has recently been called "the arrogance of humanism," by which is meant the self-important transfer of religious power to the power of mind, itself a form of rescue fantasy. At the very least, contemporary students — more than their teachers — have little respect for the secular religion of humanism. With a vengeance many have turned back to a fundamentalism as strident as the leftist anti-rationalism of two decades ago. Yet although many may feel saved, they do not, in my observation, feel or act strong. In 1973 Allen Grossman wrote:

> Poems are occasions of the greatness of persons. Conceived of as great objects, they become the tombs of possibility for generations and obstacles to the meditative self-recovery of individuals, obstacles which are ipso facto insuperable. The impoverishment of poems as meditative tools at present is apparent in the resort of the young to heterogeneous quasi-religious meditative disciplines. Greatness, when it seems to derive from the object alone, is a phantom from which it is consistent with dignity to flee.[11]

A major effort in my course has been to impress upon my students the need to look at literature as an effectual language. The goal of literary study ought to be praxis, a synergism of reflection and action. Indeed, I have been amazed by how seriously many students, raised in the heartless gobble of language offered by television and advertising, rallied with this goal — moreover, how relieved they were to hear it. As Lionel Trilling said of the way one should read language in works of art (and, I would add, in all language): "these structures [of modern literature] were not pyramids or triumphal arches, they were manifestly contrived to be not static and commemorative but mobile and aggressive, and one does not describe a quinquereme or a howitzer or a tank without estimating how much *damage* it can

11. Allen Grossman, "Criticism, Consciousness, and the Sources of Life: Some Tasks for English Studies," in *Uses of Literature,* ed. Monroe Engel (Cambridge: Harvard University Press, 1973), 43.

do."[12] This means that Wordsworth revised his "Ode" on the basis of certain known pressures, not simply in order to make it "better." It means that reviewers and nineteenth-century critics made judgments about the poem, judgments not about its quality but about whether or not it was *true* according to their political and religious as well as artistic points of view. Then, in the same vein, I asked my students to evaluate and judge particulars in the poem, and I asked them to revise their own writing, not solely to make it "better" but to correct failures in argument and incorrect perceptions and, most of all, to take the opportunity to revise their thinking. Instead of writing yet another "disinterested" analysis of a poem, they began to take on the challenge of committed evaluation, to enter their (rather, *our*) versions of the controversies around the "Ode" that had enspirited Coleridge and Hazlitt. I asked them to risk their receptivity to literature as consoling beauty through a recovery of as much context as a semester would allow. "What for me is the fate of beauty?" was a question asked eventually by many of the students. Let me now set forth the context in its details.

The formal study of English and American Literature at the University of Colorado begins with English 200, at one time called "Critical Writing," now "Writing about Literature." Allowing for a range of teaching techniques, literary preferences, and theoretical convictions, one can expect English 200 to include weekly writing assignments and presentations — often from an anthology — of many works covering the major accepted literary genres. Instructors will sometimes include classic examples of literary criticism. The class never exceeds twenty students, so discussion is not only possible but required. The students are primarily sophomores although one will often find some freshmen and a smattering of juniors and seniors who have "put off" the course in the vain hope of not having to take it. Although there are other area requirements, English 200 is the only required course in the major. The department, through this course, places upon the

12. Lionel Trilling, *Beyond Culture* (New York: Harcourt Brace Jovanovich, 1979), 13.

students the stamp of its vision of literature and a sense of the procedures and habits of mind appropriate for English Studies. Into this setting I introduced my revision of this course.

The only primary text of the course was Wordsworth's "Ode," in its authorized version in Ernest de Selincourt's edition of the poetry. This is essentially the version read after 1820, by the Victorians, moderns, and ourselves, the one anthologized for our students and commented upon by our critics. During several weeks of close study of this anthology piece the students followed as closely as possible the reasoning of the poet, entering into the world of his images and his values, the "codes" of Wordsworth and the Romantics. They then turned to a chronologically ordered selection of odes from Pindar and Horace through the Renaissance and the eighteenth century to Coleridge and slightly beyond Wordsworth's "Ode" to the odes of Shelley and Keats. This was the beginning of the discovery of the limits to Wordsworth's "originality," the generically predetermined character of his poem. Put differently, they began to pinpoint the moments of tension in the "Ode" between commitment to the tradition and commitment to its rethinking. From here they explored a different kind of tension — that of commitment to different versions of the poem. They studied Jared Curtis's variorum texts in the Cornell Wordsworth Series *Poems, in Two Volumes,* [13] which included not only all variants from manuscripts through all lifetime editions but also facsimiles of manuscripts and their transcriptions. We also considered the title page and the location of the poem in the book of its first publication and how these things might affect one's reading of the poem in its original and subsequent settings. A study of manuscript changes and the revisions of published versions led naturally to and was interwoven with discussion of biography and English and European history. This did not produce the usual effect of, as it is called, "background material," because by this time it was becoming impossible to think in terms of background and foreground. The poem was becom-

13. William Wordsworth, *Poems, in Two Volumes, and Other Poems, 1800–1807,* ed. Jared Curtis (Ithaca: Cornell University Press, 1983).

ing knotted in a set of patterns and influences, pressures from history, the psyche, biography, and the constraints of literary form and tradition. At this point students engaged the early nineteenth-century reviewers and two major critical contemporaries, Coleridge and particularly Hazlitt, knotting the poem even more in controversy and politics. Nineteenth-century readers of the "Ode" usually asked not what the poem *meant* but whether or not it was true and consequential. G. M. Hopkins went so far as to declare that the "Ode" ranked nearly as high in the consequential events of civilization as Plato and Christ. Thus truth in the "Ode" came to the poem not as an event of consciousness or sincerity but rather as an assertion of ideas. Along with this I presented other contemporary ideas about the same subjects, particularly about childhood, human development, the place of passion and sex in human life, and Enlightenment and counter-Enlightenment valuations of reasoning and questioning. In this light students read selections from Rousseau's *Emile,* from Paine and Burke and Blake and Wollstonecraft. Finally I further contextualized the "Ode" with poems from *Lyrical Ballads,* the 1807 *Poems, in Two Volumes,* the 1800 *Preface,* and parts of *The Prelude.*

As I tried to enforce the idea of context, effectuality, and evaluation in the reading of the poem, I asked the same of my students. For most of the paper topics I asked them fundamentally to evaluate rather than fundamentally to analyze (although analysis was inevitably part of their work). We also tried to define in minute detail the audience for whom they were writing, an audience — namely, me and them — who knew both the poem and the conditions under which we were reading it. Each paper could be revised two or three times; examples of each version were presented to the class. At the same time they kept a weekly journal on the poem and class discussion in order to highlight by contrast the requirements of heavily contextualized writing (with its demands of logical thinking) with a more intimate form. Yet it became clear that even intimacy in writing must be learned.

But who were these students? And what did this syllabus imply for them? They were, first of all, adolescents. I slowly recognized that this fact determined much of their response to

Wordsworth-in-context and, as I became more conscious of what it might mean to teach — specifically — adolescents, it determined the emphasis of my own teaching. Furthermore, they were adolescents at the University of Colorado — a good, if uneven, state university in the western United States. And they were studying in the mid-1980s, a decade — perhaps too generally put — of reaction. Many students are Coloradans; but many are not, traveling from both coasts, the Midwest, and Texas to attend college in a beautiful (if increasingly suburban and "high tech") small city at the foot of the Rocky Mountains. Not surprisingly, the student body is largely middle or upper-middle class, tending toward political conservatism and religious fundamentalism though not (at least in my presence) oppressively doctrinaire. The vast majority of students are white.

These students, again to speak generally, do not see *mind* as the most powerful of instruments, or at least they do not see themselves as mentally superior persons. Nor do they see themselves as the next generation of intellectual elite; they have little desire to acquire such a position. They are not well read and generally have poor-to-adequate high school preparation in thinking and writing. From time to time at the end of this course individuals voice their anger at the poverty of their secondary education and at their parents' blindness about education at home. Yet by and large my colleagues and I enjoy teaching them. For they are responsive, articulate, and imaginative, and they learn and usually display personal self-confidence. Historically they become solid and sometimes notable contributors to our society. Most aim toward the secure vocations: law, medicine, and above all business. (Although I think this portrait faithfully acknowledges an "average" student, it hardly does justice to the range of individuals.)

These students, it should follow from my portrait, are not notably self-conscious or historically conscious. It is a rare student who finds the historical past a tangible counterweight to the present. Much, one guesses, is repressed or absent or at best nascent. For my particular set of students, therefore, I have derived a course that envisions a poem — to alter Plato's parable of the cave—as a shadow cast from personal, ideological, sexual, historical, textual, and literary-generic "drives." It is a course in the repressed materials of what otherwise appears to the student as a disembodied comfort.

It took over two years of working out this course before I began to realize that the syllabus just recounted and the issues raised by the "Ode" engaged in a particularly sensitive way the students' own psychosexual context: adolescence. Revision, both in Wordsworth's poem and in their own writing, encouraged self-consciousness and self-scrutiny which, however, were largely socially determined. The uncovering of erotic fantasy in suppressed material in the "Ode" spoke to this tender area of adolescent experience, the desire for and the fear of the erotic life. An initial immersion in Wordsworth's rhetoric of transcendence and consolation, followed by a critical evaluation of it, made the students more aware of their own adolescent "rescue fantasies," the wish that something in the environment would assert for them the power of certainty and safety amidst their own "identity confusions." They saw that "imitation" ("Ode," section 7), a highly exercised faculty in the child, led to a deeper identification with the members and institutions of society; a fact that Wordsworth—just as they might—seemed intellectually to deplore but emotionally to embrace. They saw that "obstinate questioning" seemed at once a transgression, an illegitimate probing of and into the world, and yet their birthright—a gesture of their own power to widen the limits to their control. And as adolescents (perhaps more than the exploring oedipal child) they considered that all these acts of mind were powerful precisely because they touch and affect the lives of others. These, of course, include poetry itself, and especially *this* poem, seemingly insulated by contemplation yet imagining and moulding a particular audience to live and act with its principles and preferences before them.

I find the power of art mysterious — or, rather, I should say *powers*, since art touches me through several apparently divergent faculties. To say, as I did in the preceding chapter, that I have moved from a New Critical humanism to a belief in education as the development of a critical consciousness — from an apolitical to a more political relationship to art — describes one effect of my experience with art but hardly describes the experiences themselves. Indeed, as I recall the spots of artistic time in my life, the moments of being in art, I find that on the one hand art-as-consolation has a much deeper and earlier source than my formal literary education; on the other hand the seeds of my more political response to art are also not new. Let me recapitulate some of that history (recognizing that art alone cannot account for the formation of one's choices and convictions). The fact that in adolescence my particular susceptibility to New Criticism — so prevalent among literature instructors of my generation — was borne of an earlier moment in American intellectual life may be of some use to readers of a book in which the lives of teacher, students, and text converge.

My grandfather, the poet Melville Cane, and his wife, the art teacher Florence Cane, spent their middle years in the 1920s participating in that group of artist-intellectuals that included Waldo Frank, Lewis Mumford, Alfred Stieglitz, Van Wyck Brooks, Marsden Hartley, Arthur Dove, and so on. Melville Cane, by profession a copyright lawyer, knew, in that capacity, important American poets and novelists of the period. Both Melville and Florence Cane were stimulated by Freud and Jung when psychoanalysis first hit America, and both had Jungian analyses; both — particularly my grandmother — saw analysis as an adventure in personal liberation of "the self" and extended their enthusiasms to those currently fashionable doctors of the soul (or, as Gorham Munson called them, "black-sheep philosophers") Gurdjieff, Orage, and Ouspensky. Florence Cane, along with her sister Margaret Naumburg (usually considered the pioneer theorist of art therapy in this country), immediately turned these visions of personal liberation toward education and founded and developed the famous Walden School in New York City. My grandmother's book, aptly entitled *The Artist in Each of Us* (1951, rev. 1983), was a theory of art education based upon aiding the pupil — by exercises and thoughtful encouragement — to inform artistic ideas and images with unconscious or at least natural energies. Margaret Naumburg extended these principles beyond the realm of the normal individual's repression of drives to the realm of pathological repressions and distortions, so that the function of artistic activity became for her single-mindedly therapeutic.

My grandfather's poetry, at its most characteristic, also worked from the same psychodynamic hypothesis about art and mind: art can and should release the pent-up unconscious forces blocking one's fulfillment into a harmony of inner and outer states — a condition defining, for him, mental health. Essentially a pastoral hypothesis, many of his poems elaborate this psychodrama in natural imagery:

BEES, AFTER RAIN

Dormant, their house sodden with rain,
Stunned by sudden sun,
The bees stir, revive,
Charge wildly out of the hive,
Race
Furiously,

Then gloriously
Interlace
A golden skein.

AT THIS UNLIKELY HOUR

Embers crumble
Mauve to ashen,
Dust of passion
Snows the hearth.

Now the hearth's a grave,
Save for an unsuspected spark
That lurks and circumvents the dark,
And bursts to flower
At this unlikely hour.

For both of my grandparents, Jung's conviction about the ir-
radiating power of unconscious, determining images formed the
core of their professional and vocational commitments. Behind
Jung stands perhaps the greatest of all Romantic theorists of self
in its relationship to a repressive modern society, Friedrich Schiller.
Florence Cane quotes Schiller in a headnote to one of her chapters: "As soon as it is light in man, it is no longer night without."
The Jungian dramatization of this occurs in *Psychological Types*
where Prometheus, the bringer of fire and light, is seen as a "suffering god within," a figure to be saved and nurtured in order to
bring enlightenment. As my grandparents saw it, directly in the
Romantic tradition, the liberation of the self through art meant,
potentially, the liberation of oppressed classes or races.

Yet a side of this legacy has become for me problematic: in
his lovely poet's autobiography and guide book, *Making a Poem*
(1953) — much of which I heard in conversation while growing
up — Melville Cane emphasizes "detachment" as the state of mind
necessary for creative work. Who can argue with this? Psychoanalysis requires detachment; coming to recognize the immense
power of the transference demands a rigorous application of the
spirit of detachment. Originally much of the socially radical artistic programs of the 1920s relied upon it. Out of detachment

one not only could release the language of the unconscious but could release the images of suppressed people and races and the suppressed second sex. And yet in art, detachment in the act of creation too often seems to lead to detachment in the vision put forth by the work of art: the mind in the work and subsequently in the viewer or reader ceases to function except to record its wonderment. The mind loses its desire to question and explore, to test vision positively against social reality; both the mind and its object — beauty — grow chaste. (In the instance of my grandfather — if I may speak critically of one who was enormously important to my early thinking about such matters — this chasteness of mind led him, I believe, to overvalue both the image and also the word that embodied it. Words at times became for him a fetish, leading to the undervaluation of ideas.)

Once this inversion of priorities is accepted, it is just a short leap to the embrace of something that at first seems quite different: New Criticism and its more recent elaborations. For here mind turns inward upon the object of criticism, and after agreeing to limit thought to the thought (or the vocabulary of the thought) of the poet, mind exchanges its own freedom for the exercise and notice of the internal relations of the poem. New Critical reading is an act of submission to the thought of another by making the words of the poet more important than his ideas.

But the major statements of the New Critical humanist pioneers — e.g., Brooks, Tate, Blackmur — do not reflect a wish to deny thought; and surely they write with an eye always on the social and cultural condition of the modern individual. Interestingly, however, they too value detachment from or transcendence of the modern commercial world through poetry; they value "aesthetic education" as the means of becoming more "human." Their essentialism reflects their belief in a human self beyond history; literature is at best a form of pastoral — immutable, imperturbable, consoling.

My Harvard education in literature began and ended with exercises in pastoral. I began with a seminar in the Eclogues of Virgil (my father vainly but correctly pleading: why don't you study philosophy or international relations instead of counting flower images in Latin poems?) and a course in Romanticism commencing with the conversation poems of Coleridge. College ended with an honors thesis on the Christianization of the Catullan *carpe diem* tradition in Renaissance France and England. In this latter I unwittingly (from the present perspective) showed that I had learned the lessons of Harvard perfectly: what's to be preferred is not experience but rather the spiritualization and internalization of experience, of erotic love and desire.

The consoling view of literature is very powerful and valuable. To the extent that it offers monuments of coherence and hope, it serves us well. But when a reader imagines that beauty in art demands for its existence society's "bad present" from which to escape, then it has ceased to function positively. I cannot know the entire path of release from my hunger for literary consolation (partly because it has not fully abated and, I am sure, never will), but there are moments which will have to stand for the whole. I noticed first of all a change both in the kinds of art I came to like and a change in what I saw and thought when I looked at or read it.

In 1968 I read for the first time Thomas Mann's *Dr. Faustus,* a book that revolutionized my concept of what literature could do. As I watched Mann's composer-hero Adrian Leverkuhn grow up amidst an atmosphere of traditional musical harmonies, but mature as a composer amidst one of dissonance and strain, I was forced to consider that "beauty"—in the sense of the harmoniously coherent—was historically conditioned and limited and not universal or timeless. I remember too a feeling of excitement at discovering in this novel the immediate importance not only of history but of ideas: Goethe, Schiller, Schopenhauer, Nietzsche, Beethoven, Wagner, Schönberg, as well as Luther, alchemy, and the medieval and Renaissance Faust tradition. The life and music of Adrian Leverkuhn had a precarious power—full of mystery and isolation, a thing unto itself, and yet seemingly wholly determined by a variety of histories and traditions. The strange mixture of immutability and influence in the midst of modern cataclysms produced an art of defiant, tortuously complex freedom and a personal life that veered off toward self-concentration, madness, and finally death.

How did this affect my thinking about the unit of beauty: the image? In *Dr. Faustus* the image only rarely consoles; instead it, like Leverkuhn himself, becomes highly abstracted, disembodied; its beauty increases rather than decreases the reader's awareness of its distance from reality. Similarly, a painting by Manet focused much of my thinking about the power of the image to seduce the observer or reader away from thought. A young woman dressed in pale blue stands *Before the Mirror,* face and body away from the viewer. Her reflection just appears from one edge of the mirror. I have always been drawn toward this picture out of desire for what is barely suggested. But not long ago, visiting this painting at the Guggenheim Museum in New York, I determined that the point of the mirror was to comment on the nature of the image, that the image could trap desire in imagery itself. Like Leverkuhn's music, the celestial light of this woman's apparel marks the image of her, and perhaps of all imagery, as being a thing apart from reality; for the viewer who accepts the primacy of imagery, imagery becomes a self-preoccupation leading nowhere. This to me is the "idea" of *Before the Mirror;* or rather Manet has occasioned that idea in me, a fact which draws me even closer to this superb painting.

The writers about literature and culture who have more recently influenced me (such as Trilling, Adorno, Benjamin, Foucault) are those who tend to concern themselves more with ideas and history than with language and who tend to accord a radical, not consolatory, status to the image. Generally left-wing politically, they tend to look at literature as manifestations of the power relations at work in modern society, and as such they show concern for suppressed or repressed elements, such as (illicit) sexual desire and minority or lower classes. They also try to analyze the assumptions by which the dominant class operates. This approach in turn has affinities with psychoanalysis since it too is concerned with repression (of drives) and the analysis of one's assumed patterns of thought and behavior. For someone, like myself, who has undergone a psychoanalysis, the task, I think, is to keep the analytic function alive while not denying the radical dignity of the image. Psychoanalytic reductionism in poetic interpretation simply substitutes the effects — seduction and consolation — of one image system (psychoanalysis) for the original one. At the same time I have found myself wondering (perhaps naively): how can a personal psychoanalysis not extend the exercise of self-scrutiny toward social systems of repression? Now, as a teacher, I am trying to bring this subtle critical consciousness into the education of my students. After concluding this introductory section by remarking upon revision as the general principle (in the course) both of self-scrutiny and historical criticism, I will show how the students begin the process of critical consciousness amidst their embrace of the consoling language and structure of Wordsworth's monumental "Immortality Ode."

3　Two Minds about Revision

Revision: what is it? I asked the students this question at the beginning of the term. As often happened, their answers ranged from consideration of revision they might do to that of revision as they imagined its place in the activity of immortal poets. The former—at this early moment—was only hypothetical and filled them with a collective terror. The thought of serious self-revision, with the help of peers and teacher, seemed to relate to the excessive privacy of sexual fantasy and experience. The latter turned out to be far more threatening: poets revise because of the a priori teleology of their work. A poem strives for a single outcome, known or unknown to its poet. The Ur-poem grows according to its predetermined instructions. The poet is only the agent of this subterranean current. With this last image the writing of the poet and of the student merge: all good writing "flows." The process is natural, unmediated; an ideal would probably be so-called automatic writing. Any need for revision in poetry is only proof of the imperfectness of the poet: the poem, the artifact, belongs to God; it is eternal, uncontaminated.

Early versions of a paper or a poem are finally judged to exist only as a process, or better, a progression. Judged negatively, the early version has no substantive content; it is only means to an end, which in a sense has already been judged as perfect and pure. One applies the understanding to an early version

29

only as an instrument of negation: x is to be excluded, modified. Early versions obediently self-destruct or erase themselves from the memory of the reader except insofar as they confirm the teleology and the authority of the final version. One applies the understanding to a final version of a paper in order to reach it. One applies the understanding to a poem as an instrument of secondary power: the primary act of mind is worship, the secondary is analysis for the sake of binding the individual to the object of worship.

What is revision? They said it was (1) clarification, (2) correction, (3) amplification, (4) concision. An authoritative text requires somewhere a figure of authority. Writing is improvement toward a norm; the text is judged negatively: it is not clear, correct, elaborate, or concise enough. A first version exists in order to be improved. No wonder the terror: a first version by definition will not meet the standards. But in the fantasy of the student, writing under this censure means that his or her thought is negated. And similarly the early version of a poem contains no thought and no commitments.[1] Neither poem nor paper is a social act, a belief which leads to a vision of alienation and loneliness for both student and poet.

That such fantasies prevail in many young people engaged in literary study does not mean that in practice one cannot help a student "improve" or "clarify" his or her writing, but it does mean that the student can (and should) be urged to see obscu-

---

1. A recent writer on the nature of revision in literature — Hershel Parker, *Flawed Texts and Verbal Icons* (Evanston: Northwestern University Press, 1984) — has explored the problem of the authority of the final text. But his understanding, rather than finally rehistoricizing the work, only shifts the site of authority from the latest version to the earliest. His view is very Romantic and Shelleyan: the closer one gets to the moment of inspired composition, the closer one gets to the authoritative version. Revisions — often a product of tamer thinking, "second thoughts," publishers' demands, reviewers' criticisms — tarnish the original brightness. (See, for example, pp. 2–4.) Revision, in other words, doesn't make things "better"; it makes things "worse." Parker does not, however, entertain the possibility that revision may make things *different* and that one activity of historical criticism may worthily be the discovery of the pressures working upon a writer in the act of revision.

rity in writing as a conflict among different ways of understanding the object, as the internalized censorship of the extent or boldness of thinking about the subject. The point is to insist upon the positive content of the student's thinking. In this sense the word processor — if not carefully understood — is an agent of Romantic ideology, for it does not preserve early versions; one cannot look at the erasure or the cross-out; they vanish before what is at once always the authoritative version. Composing on a word processor is always a game of power.

Something similar applies to the poet's early versions: as one student, weeks into the study of Wordsworth eventually and triumphantly observed in his notebook: "Reading all the corrections and changes makes me think that Wordsworth was writing too many poems at once."

I endeavored to show my students that revisions ought to be recognized, more fruitfully, as a change or modification of point of view, a change or modification of commitment. Such a recognition, I hoped, would serve to grant greater dignity and authenticity to thought at any moment and, I hope (as utopian as it may sound), will continue to serve well their own commitments to the instrumentality of critical thinking. The student quoted above, though resistant to the possibility that the poet's revisions come down to the making of fundamental choices, has nonetheless made this admission and thus has opened himself to the same choice-making in his activity as a critic. Clearly, he understands by *choice* that for him and the poet it cannot have meaning in narrowly aesthetic terms that would not mean *choice* at all but *improvement,* making the poem better. Choice refers to the condition of life itself, of experience that is socially, historically, and psychologically determined and interpreted. Mimesis may describe the essential nature of poetry, but the acts of poetic and critical choice imitate nothing, nor are they nothing; they are for the critic the thing itself.

Part Two
Wordsworth's "Ode": Examining Its Convictions

4   A Message from Eternity

Part of the difficulty in presenting this course was with myself.
The first time I taught it, I capitulated during the final weeks
to what Geoffrey Hartman once called "the divinatory mode" of
the poem, to the healing effects of Wordsworthian beauty; its
consoling organization or momentum prevailed along with my
own fear of denying the students their own classroom consolation. All the dialectics of ideology and experience seemed to shrink
before divinity, or rather, those dialectics — it turned out — existed
to bring the divinatory gleam back into prominence. Why could
I not, like a good psychoanalyst, maintain discomfort to the very
end — the discomfort, in this case, of "cultural criticism?" In Walter Benjamin's term, I restored the "aura" or distancing illusions
of classical art. I recall now the lure to me of "the beautiful," the
power of the divinatory mode in this poem when I was prepar-
ing, the second time, to give the course and specifically to intro-
duce the young people to the poem by reading it out loud:

> Reading the "Ode" out loud, I am yet again overwhelmed. It is
> yet again a journey, an immersion. Each section, read slowly,
> seems like an epoch, one of the ages of man. Reading it aloud,
> it does seem like a missive from eternity, "sent in apt admonish-
> ment," and I find myself drawn to emphasize this, its otherness,
> the "alien sound." In the classroom I must begin here. We begin

with the impact of that eternal message. I also feel its relentless-
ness, nearly sadistic in its intensity, as I read to myself, I come
upon "those first affections" and slow down; the words settle into
consciousness, begin to spread out onto the lake of the mind in
repose, when the syntax demands the next modification, "those
shadowy recollections": affections/recollections, feelings plunged
into shadowy memory: the modesty of "recollection" in a poem
of vision! But the poem then drives on before these rhymes can
form their own poem: "be they what they may." So the poet does
not know what they are; yet the deathly weight and rhyme of
those monosyllables scattering precision immediately coalesce into
a new idea, a "light," fountain-light or master-light, a source from
below, from nature or power from above, from the human and
the divine.

Relentlessly, I am dragged through one such event after another. Meaning or meanings accumulate in such detail, all press-
ing upon each other, with such power over me. Would I fall down
into the dizzy/gentle fields of sleep and know in oblivion!

The next day I read the poem to the class, performed it in
a heightened and not wholly human voice. Some found that the
reading made it more of an event or happening. They said, upon
hearing it, that the poet wanted to "share" his findings with us.
I had not expected to hear about intimacy.

Others saw this personalizing from the reading as a defect,
not in the poem but in my act of reading it. The reading had
reduced the infinity of possible readings. The poem, for those
persons, exists in eternity through which voice and community
had pierced. One said that I had made the poem more somber.
This made me uncomfortable but led me to reflect (to myself)
upon the depth of loss in the poem. But loss as poetic theme
resonated to loss in poetic experience, or the fantasy of such experience. The voice had made the poem available to an audience
— the students became this audience which, at that moment unknown to them or to me, had had thrust upon them the burden
but also the exhilaration of authentic response. Through voice
the poem's apparently unassailable authority was shaken. If I had
attempted to speak with the consoling otherness of eternity, I

had intimated to these young people their subjecthood and their visibility to each other and to me. "Poems are occasions of the greatness of persons." There were those who seemed to shrink before the spoken "Ode," but for others the reading became a gateway to their own dignity as readers.

5   A Poem of Contemplation

We began the course by reading the "Ode" through the "codes" of the poem. Wordsworth's "Ode" is a poem of contemplation, of the inner life; by contrast, the outer world is far less sharply etched. What does this mean? It has an exquisite regard for inner states: changes of mood, descent to mourning, ascent to ecstasy, levelings out to comfort and assurance; for registerings of perception: recognition of losses, formulations of human development and of development as fundamentally tragic, a reversal of the understanding about this formulation of life, a reformulation of life as bound in a healthful way to the natural world:

> To me alone there came a thought of grief:
> A timely utterance gave that thought relief,
>   And I again am strong:
>   . . . .
> No more shall grief of mine the season wrong;
> . . . .
>
> The fullness of your bliss, I feel — I feel it all.
>   Oh evil day! if I were sullen
>   While Earth herself is adorning,
>   This sweet May-morning,
>   . . . .
>   I hear, I hear, with joy I hear!
>   — But there's a Tree, of many, one,

A single Field which I have looked upon,
Both of them speak of something that is gone:
. . . .

> O joy! that in our embers
> Is something that doth live,
> That nature yet remembers
> What was so fugitive!

The thought of our past years in me doth breed
Perpetual benediction: . . .
. . . .

Then sing, ye Birds, sing, sing a joyous song!

And O, ye Fountains, Meadows, Hills, and Groves,
Forebode not any severing of our loves!
. . . .

To me the meanest flower that blows can give
Thoughts that do often lie too deep for tears.

The poem, as well as the metaphor for development within the poem, appears as an odyssey with its attendant perilous crises of encounter. Yet one must immediately qualify this description with the word "internal." This is not quite the same thing as a "spiritual odyssey," since there one inevitably experiences the external world as a substantial thing; but in the "Ode" the outer world seems strangely absent in a way that the setting of the poem and speaker would not predict. Surrounded by flowers, lambs, birds, cataracts, winds—a host of nature's sights and melodies—and from time to time addressing children, the speaker nonetheless and at the same time seems surrounded only by his words. The flurry of emotional, perceptual, and cognitive changes comes from nowhere, is not actually touched by the world. This poem of inner states is correspondingly marked by exclusions, absences, and an outer world that is never quite palpable.

The point has been made often that several objects in the poem lack references that seem called for: What was the "thought of grief"? what was the "timely utterance"? what is the "Tree, of many, one"? and the "single Field" that "speak of something that is gone"? what are the "first affections" and "shadowy recollec-

tions"? and what are the "Thoughts that do often lie too deep
for tears"? When at the end of section IV the poet asks what
Trilling calls the "terrible questions,"

> Whither is fled the visionary gleam?
> Where is it now, the glory and the dream?

the vanishings could be said to apply as well to the whole external world. And Wordsworth's late annotation for the poem may
refer to this basic absence:

> . . . I was often unable to think of external things as having ex-
> ternal existence, and I communed with all that I saw as some-
> thing not apart from, but inherent in, my own immaterial na-
> ture. Many times while going to school have I grasped at a wall
> or tree to recall myself from this abyss of idealism to the reality.[1]

For all the prominence of mood changes and references to sullen-
ness and to joy, affective reality and fantasy also seem strangely
unavailing. The epigraph sets the conditions: "And I *could*
wish. . . ." The possibility, the capacity to wish stands in place
of the actual wish or fantasy.[2]

The wish itself is formulated with enormous care, an analysis
of which reveals an impossibility in experience. For what is "natural piety"? "Piety" implies the choice or will to submit to a divine
order, and thereby a knowledge of a life lived without piety. But
"natural," particularly in the late eighteenth-century world view,
implies innocence, that the order exists outside or without reference to the human will. The binding, or covenant, is born not
out of God's and man's willed agreement. The covenant exists
between "days," not willing beings: "And I could wish my days
to be / Bound each to each by natural piety." This fantasy not

---

1. Wordsworth, *Poetical Works* ed. Ernest de Selincourt and Helen Darbishire (Oxford: Clarendon, 1958), 4:463.
2. Cf. Freud's phrase in a letter to Fliess (May 4, 1896), "unbewusste Sehn-
suchtabsicht" (unconscious intention of longing).

fantasized but just formulated, lives, finally, only in language. Moreover, the students appreciated the nineteenth-century editor's error:

> The Winds come to me from the fields of *sheep*

instead of the accurate reading:

> The Winds come to me from the fields of *sleep*.

The error restores the line to experience, but the actual line cuts off reference to create a beautiful but nonreferential line. That the poem turns away *both* from reference to the external world and from fantasy suggests something about the nature of fantasy to which we will later return: it usually requires a clear acknowledgment of the external world.

Even the divine, hovering incessantly around the edges of the poem, seems impalpable. God, except for in section V, only enters through "intimation." Many of the young people in the class, hungry for religious certitudes, fed on the Bible, which — in comparison with their ignorance in most of the thought and literature of Western Civilization — they possess in hypertrophied form, hone in on these intimations, seeking confirmation of their often rigidly conceived narratives of fall and redemption. The Biblical narrative, branded with fire on their imaginations, organizes any susceptible artifact to its specifications. The poem, they said, is "cyclical" in its presentation of an Eden, a fall, and a recovery. God is the ever-seeing "eye" of section XI:

> The Clouds that gather round the setting sun
> Do take a sober colouring from an eye
> That hath kept watch o'er man's mortality;

The "faith that looks through death" means both that the poem attempts to come to terms with death and that the poet learns the reality of an "after-life." The power of these intimations, taken as presence when in fact they are far less palpable, can be shown not only through the particular contemporary avidity for religious explanation and consolation but also through its being the stock-and-trade critical reading of the poem from the Victorian era to the very recent past.[3] And yet the hard evidence for the presence of theology in the poem is by and large wanting (compared, for example, to other Wordsworth poems of the period, e.g., "Ode to Duty" and "Character of the Happy Warrior").

Religion is not very substantial; nor is the poet's own sense of loss. He claims the reality of a loss of something, but the words "gleam," "glory," and "dream" (section IV) hardly crystallize what the something is. Moreover, as one student observed, the poet seems to learn of this loss by report and by what oddly seems like fiction: "Both [the Tree and the Field] *speak* of something that is gone: / The Pansy at my feet / Doth the same *tale* repeat: . . ." While such proof of mediation of experience through language may be a source of delight to deconstructionist readers, to my students it became a source of uneasiness and of (fascinating, to be sure) irritation and disbelief. For those with religious predilections, the poem literally enthralled them, that is, held them captive to the anticipation of Christian heroism and comfort but did not satisfy the hunger. It demanded consent without ever fully giving evidence of the poet's commitment to his moods, his losses and gains, his doctrine, his questions and his answers or solutions. This moment in the course was eerie, vaguely menacing. The students seemed caught between the continuum of conventional responses to literature and sincere wishes for salvation, and a warily stated skepticism about the reality of the poet's experience. For no matter how strong their need for a structure confirmatory to belief was, their need to respond to something "real" was at least as strong. One student said, tentatively and uncynically, that the consoling language of sections IX to XI seemed "painted on," "creating hope where hope didn't exist." Without declaring it, some of these students were begin-

3. See, for an example of a recent consoling reading, Helen Vendler, "Lionel Trilling and the *Immortality Ode,*" *Salmagundi* 41 (1978): 66–86.

ning to entertain the possibility that the "Ode" exhibited life as the appearance of life. For the moment the initial thrill of discovering the "Ode"'s power may have seemed hollow; the poem may have appeared to con them (for what reason?) into false joy and enthusiasm.

A person asks a question in order to make the world more real. Questions are critically important in the "Ode," as well as in other poems by Wordsworth and the Romantics generally. But for Wordsworth and others the question and the questioner maintain a particular ambiguity about answers and external reality. The most startling and to me unexpected discussion during the first six weeks occurred around the mention, in section IX, of the child as a questioning "Creature":

> Not for these [things "most worthy to be blest"] I raise
> The song of thanks and praise;
> But for those obstinate questionings
> Of sense and outward things,
> Fallings from us, vanishings;
> Blank misgivings of a Creature
> Moving about in worlds not realised,
> High instincts before which our mortal Nature
> Did tremble like a guilty Thing surprised.

I asked them what the word "Creature" brought to mind in this passage. Immediately they associated to "Frankenstein," to monsters, to wild animals. No one thought more simply or literally of "Creature" as the work of the Creator (as the capital C might suggest, and as one might have expected from this group heavily indoctrinated in and inclined toward Biblical associations); nor did anyone refer back to that earlier moment when, poised in the midst of laughing nature, the poet calls out: "Ye blessèd Creatures! I have heard the call / Ye to each other make." Children, animals, plants all are the happy results of a Creator who saw that his work was good. Each creature projects and echoes back its happiness to all the others. The students did not make the connection not because they did not see one "Creature" transformed into the other but because they did not perceive the two creatures to be of the same species. The first is a creature of an ideology that declares the child's proximity to nature, its essential innocence; the second defines the child in starkly human terms: it is the questioner.

Encouraging these associations, I asked them to consider in what sense the questioning child might be monstrous and deformed and an outlaw. I also suggested that — if one followed the Frankenstein association — the Creature was a creation not of God but of man, one who transgressed moral, to say nothing of scientific, limits. Moreover, I offered the traditional allusions in this passage to Satan guiltily entering Paradise, the abode of Adam and Eve — the first human creatures — guiltily eating of the tree of knowledge. And the mention of guilt called up the famous *Hamlet* allusion to a ghost who, at the approach of day, "started like a guilty thing." Before we had even talked about questioning, they had imprinted it with nightmarish, negatively judgmental, and subversive meanings, meanings so severe that they ambushed, disfigured, and isolated the physical figure of the questioner. The world of the questioner, too, had changed, no longer nurturing and confirming in its pastoralism; the act of questioning seemed to produce the emptiness of, as Trilling says, "worlds not yet made real."[1] "Questionings" may be equivalent to or they may produce "fallings" and "vanishings." For the child of section IV motion and energy are the direct outcome of joy and com-

1. Lionel Trilling, "The Immortality Ode," in *The Liberal Imagination* (New York: Harcourt Brace Jovanovich, 1979).

panionship and affirmation; here the movement of the questioning child is unconnected to a feeling state and then apparently
unconnected to the child itself: it is a thoroughly alien being.

Deaf to the poem's resonance between the earlier and the later
Creatures, the students also missed the fact that the poet's meditation is organized around the "terrible" questions of sections IV
and VIII, that therefore his joy in the child as questioner comes
from identifying, in the meditation, with him:

> Whither is fled the visionary gleam?
> Where is it now, the glory and the dream?

> Why with such earnest pains dost thou provoke
> The years to bring the inevitable yoke,
> Thus blindly with thy blessedness at strife?

It seemed that the passage, perhaps both for students and poet,
evoked something so compelling in its terror that for the moment no contrary vision either of questioning or of childhood
could offer consolation. Indeed, some students could never disabuse themselves of the notion that *all* of section IX evokes the
terror and despair of the questioner, even though the poet clearly
invokes the child in order partly to praise the continuity of childhood questioning in his maturity. Questioning becomes the great
gift bestowed by childhood upon adulthood. The disinterested
pastoralism of the classroom, which insists upon "perspective"
and a "balance" among viewpoints, momentarily vanished as the
students fell into fantasies of transgression and disfigurement.

The rebound, however, was quick, but the two major views
about the nature of questioning that followed revealed as much
as had the fantasies. First, the students said, questioning is in
itself a basic form of self-realization, the gaining of identity. Second, questioning produces answers, which, they said, is "peace"
(not "reality"). About these responses one can make the following points. (1) Questioning is judged by its goodness, and in the
context of the "Ode," which is a kind of fable of self-consciousness
and its resolution, the responses seek to engage the authority and
universality of the moral to the fable. The drama of this class-

room moment, however, suggests the truth of Rousseau's brilliant attack on the effect of the moral fable (*Emile*), that the child (and instinctively the adult) identifies with the transgressing figure (the fox in "The Fox and the Crow") more than with the moralizing narrator. Identification overwhelms the context. (2) Both responses evade the fantasies of transgression and disfigurement; that is, they evade the notion that questioning is a risk taking, that asking questions creates a landscape of uncertain consequence. (3) The wholeness of the individual is never disturbed. *Wholeness* itself is a concept unquestioned, standing like a sentinel or watchman (to invoke a Freudian metaphor) who protects the individual moving around in his worlds. For it becomes clear (and the poem supports this) that the "self" is not one being who at certain moments and under certain constraints and impulses chooses to question and who must live with the consequences of his questioning when he no longer questions. Both the "self-realized" individual and the "self" living in "peace" are not in fact the self-that-questions. Behind the "self" is a "Self" or God who not only insures a final peace but insures that the questions grant room for and predict peace.

This "Self" is not God, although it is God whom these young people would at this moment invoke. Moreover, the students could be said to engage a *text*—the "Ode"—and a *Text*—the Bible: the latter protects the integrity of the former. As an example, students relentlessly invoked the *nostos* to describe the movement of the poet's meditation in the "Ode." They insisted (as does the mainline tradition of criticism) that the poet "returns" to the place of his beginnings, to a mature individual's version of unity, even though the poem does not actually use the language of return. But the "Self" is entwined with the function and meaning of questioning which, in the institutional setting of the university, as Althusser says, "teaches 'know-how', but in forms which ensure *subjection to the ruling ideology* or the mastery of its 'practice.'"[2] This "Self" is the ruling ideology and the teacher its high priest. Their

2. Althusser, "Ideology and the Ideological State Apparatuses," in *Lenin and Philosophy*, trans. Ben Brewster (New York: Monthly Review Press, 1971), 133.

understanding of questioning, therefore, shows the success, to date, of their education. It reflects a "mastery" of the poem but at the same time a willingness to defer to the larger conditions of subjection, or peace.

There is a parallel way of understanding their rebound from the "terror of discontinuity,"[3] which is that the students recognize in the picture of the questioning child something not terrifying at all but actually supportive of another comforting fantasy. It must be remembered that Wordsworth derives comfort from this view of the childhood instinct for questioning. Now, the situation (repeatedly related in the eighteenth century) in which the individual finds secondary or eventual comfort in facing the unknown as a terror is the sublime. What may represent the structure of Wordsworth's poem is the discovery that the terrified feeling of engulfment and possible destruction is rescued by the realization that the power of mind is more enduring than the forces opposing the continuity of self. According to Frances Ferguson, whose brilliant analyses of the sublime have not yet received the recognition they deserve, this fantasy of salvation through mind ("the arrogance of humanism") demands for its enactment the description of the individual as an essentially solitary, contemplative being, not known or knowing and questioning through his social relations. As I said earlier, the child's questionings produce the fallings and vanishings and an unrealized world. One reason he appears unrelated to the child of section IV is that the latter (aesthetically a figure defined by the category of the "beautiful") is defined by his social relations. But the adult poet identifies through his own questionings with the sublime child (who previously in section VIII has been associated not with people but with the divinity and his prophets), a figure primarily of contemplation and subjectivity. The peace that radiates from the final three sections is established through a careful placing of the poet among elements denoting his fantasy of simultaneous omnipotence and submissiveness: the chil-

3. Geoffrey Hartman, *Wordsworth's Poetry, 1787–1814* (New Haven: Yale University Press, 1964).

dren and lambs in section X and the mountains, streams, and groves of section XI do not count, really, as "social relations," although the poet would like us to believe otherwise ("I love the Brooks / Even more than when I tripped lightly as they"), because it is a world that does not recognize the existence of adult relations and their consequences. His "love" of this world involves no admission of otherness; he controls the natural and child-filled world in fantasy the way a parent controls children — from ideally a state of benign omniscience and detachment, both of which are implied in the determining phrase, "philosophic mind." But similarly the eye that keeps watch over man's mortality speaks to a benign force watching over and controlling *him*. The students rightly observed the ambiguity of this omniscience: did the "eye" belong to the poet? to nature? to God? As with the ambiguity about "self" and "Self" there is ambiguity about "eye" and "Eye." Similarly, this creates the condition of the rescue fantasy: that what is meant is a figure outside the self assuming salvation (which is finally submission), a figure not demanding the responsibilities and complexities of adult relations. Questioning, rather than leading to answers and consequences, seems to stimulate the occasion for the sublime rescue.

The speaker's implied terror or anguish in the presence of the unknown may turn out to be a masochistic pleasure in his own solitude, in a world that he prefers to have emptied of its inhabitants, a world not unlike that described and similarly appreciated by Keats on his Grecian urn.

> Who are these coming to the sacrifice?
>   To what green altar, O mysterious priest,
> Lead'st thou that heifer lowing at the skies,
>   And all her silken flanks with garlands dressed?
> What little town by river or sea shore,
>   Or mountain-built with peaceful citadel,
>   Is emptied of this folk, this pious morn?
> And, little town, thy streets for evermore
>   Will silent be; and not a soul to tell
>   Why thou art desolate can e'er return.

The town desolate of its inhabitants seems to afford room for the poet to fill it with himself through "empathy." In Frances Ferguson's term, the poet sees the social world as "claustrophobic" and thus gains pleasure from, imaginatively, being the only presence, the only survivor. And just as Wordsworth finds — after his bout with the terror of (empathic) isolation — "love" in nature, so Keats finds "friendship" ("friend to Man") with the urn. Both of these fetishistic loves in fact rationalize the person defined by solitude and by a world — as I suggested in the previous section — without concrete reference to objects and people. Both poems support the prevalent ideology of art that asserts its preference for a mind transcendent of social relations, in which the art object activates the fantasies of the modern individual — of grandiosity and help-lessness before a benign power. Both poems achieve their comfort through a scheme of questions designed to cancel answers.

Insofar as it reflects this set of preferences in the speaker, the poem demands the same thing of the sympathetic reader. The reader must be willing to accept the nonreferentiality and therefore the insubstantiality of certain key objects or moments (the "timely utterance," the "single Field," etc.); that is, he must accept the status of the unknown and the insubstantial for objects which do not achieve definition through their unknowability and insubstantiality. This extends to the habit of mind exhibited in the poet (a habit, by the way, that can be traced in a number of Wordsworth's poems in the early 1800s). That habit occurs between sections VIII and IX. The poet asks at the end of section VIII the difficult questions about the Child's apparently tragic makeup — his willingness to exchange his heavenly origins for the prison house of custom and imitation; but then at the beginning of section IX he dissolves the question and the need for an answer with the joyous self-revelation that the premises of his questions are not really true. Although he can see no reason or source to this revelation, the reader must accept it as valid. The reader, to sum up, must accept a world where questions are not directly answered but dissolved, where objects fall away and vanish. Such an acceptance of this subjective, solitary world is not nightmarish but joyous because the speaker, seeking to affirm the self in an elemental sense, does affirm it. The joy comes from rationalizing the object world and the world of social relations as unessential and from confirming the existence and vitality of what Wordsworth in *The Prelude* (translating Rousseau in the *Confessions*) calls the "sentiment of being."

The sublime disavowal of the object world and the world of social relations through the disavowal of the question's function as an instrument for the confirmation and engagement of those worlds is a fairly common element in Wordsworth's poetry during the time of the "Ode"'s composition. The particular form—ask a question then dissolve the question or its premises—wrenches us away from the expectations of syntax to demand assent to the disavowal. One expects an answer from a question, expects that the world of questions and answers is intersubjective: the person who asks a question (professes incomplete knowledge) cannot be the one who answers it. A question implies a community of at least two. Wordsworth does not dispute this, but he does dispute the need for the question to be answered. In fact, he seems to isolate, or shelter, the question from the conditions needed for the answer. The question becomes chaste, a syntactical unit that conjoins the questioner with a permanent condition of unknowability, not in the spirit of epistemological pessimism but in the spirit of the sublime. The best demonstration of this is in "Resolution and Independence" (1802). After their greeting, the young poet and the ancient Leech-Gatherer engage in questions and answers. The poet asks him about his work, his survival not in any metaphysical or psychological sense but in a social and economic sense.

> And now a stranger's privilege I took;
> And, drawing to his side, to him did say,
> 'This morning gives us promise of a glorious day.'
>
> A gentle answer did the old Man make,
> In courteous speech which forth he slowly drew:
> And him with further words I thus bespake,
> 'What occupation do you there pursue?
> This is a lonesome place for one like you.'
> . . . .

> He told, that to these waters he had come
> To gather leeches, being old and poor:
> Employment hazardous and wearisome!
> And he had many hardships to endure:
> From pond to pond he roamed, from moor to moor;
> Housing, with God's good help, by choice or chance;
> And in this way he gained an honest maintenance.

The answer has come but is not heard or registered. The same question and answer are later repeated, but now the answer is registered not for its social content but as an elemental benign and preternatural force that rescues the poet from his confusion.

> The old Man still stood talking by my side;
> But now his voice to me was like a stream
> Scarce heard; nor word from word could I divide;
> And the whole body of the Man did seem
> Like one whom I had met with in a dream;
> Or like a man from some far region sent,
> To give me human strength, by apt admonishment.

"Resolution" and "Independence" define the condition of the sublimely confirmed being. That is, one who is "rock-like in endurance" (Trilling),[4] self-confirming in his insistence on the insignificance, in social and economic and therefore intersubjective terms, of the answer to his questions. On a simpler scale "The Solitary Reaper" (1805) works the same way.

> Will no one tell me what she sings?—
> Perhaps the plaintive numbers flow
> For old, unhappy, far-off things,
> And battles long ago:
> Or is it some more humble lay,
> Familiar matter of today?
> Some natural sorrow, loss, or pain,
> That has been, and may be again?

4. Lionel Trilling, "Mansfield Park," in *The Opposing Self* (New York: Viking, 1955), 217.

Whate'er the theme, the Maiden sang
As if her song could have no ending;
I saw her singing at her work,
And o'er the sickle bending; —
I listened, motionless and still;
And, as I mounted up the hill,
The music in my heart I bore, -
Long after it was heard no more.

The questions asked about the girl singing and reaping alone in the field, asked in social and biographical terms, are dissolved ("Whate'er the theme . . ."), so that the "music," replacing the social language, bores into the subject and redefines him in terms of himself and the fate of his feelings. In both poems the poet places in precarious balance his social and presocial or asocial perceptions of the privileged object. As we read one question must be: which kind of perception will he choose? That he does not choose the social perceptions goes against the grain. Students often ask the wonderfully simple question: why doesn't he just walk up to the reaper and ask her directly? They must finally assent to the poet's preference for, literally, innocence — not knowing — or more precisely for his preference for defining himself — in the act of questioning — as a completely subjective and sufficient self.

I have suggested that behind this acquiescence in profound subjectivity stands a rescue fantasy in the form of a "Self" which is at once an agent of salvation from without and "Mind," a faculty of the subject that rationalizes an unimportance to intersubjectivity. That my students were very committed to this instance of rescue fantasy became clear when they discussed another Romantic poem of questioning: Blake's "The Tyger." One student startled me by calling the relentless forging of question after question — each elaborating myths of transgression, exploration, social commitment, and creation — "wandering reveries and speculations." In other words, she converted the conscious constraint, the fear, the awe, the energy and urgency, the sense of confrontation and crisis, into an idyll of pleasurable unconcern. Before passing this student's interpretation off as obtuseness, one ought to consider the direction which this misreading takes. (It is, not coincidentally, the same order of misreading proposed by the "dumb" student in Trilling's "Of This Time, of That Place." The purgatorial world of "The Ancient Mariner," a world that reflects consequence, is transformed into an idyll.) Other students then began to look at the engraving of "The Tyger" which corroborated, indeed may have been the source of, the misreading.

> Tyger, Tyger, burning bright,
> In the forests of the night;
> What immortal hand or eye,
> Could frame thy fearful symmetry?
>
> In what distant deeps or skies,
> Burnt the fire of thine eyes?
> On what wings dare he aspire?
> What the hand, dare sieze the fire?
>
> And what shoulder, & what art,
> Could twist the sinews of thy heart?
> And when thy heart began to beat,
> What dread hand? & what dread feet?
>
> What the hammer? what the chain,
> In what furnace was thy brain?
> What the anvil? what dread grasp,
> Dare its deadly terrors clasp?
>
> When the stars threw down their spears
> And water'd heaven with their tears:
> Did he smile his work to see?
> Did he who made the Lamb make thee?
>
> Tyger Tyger burning bright,
> In the forests of the night:
> What immortal hand or eye,
> Dare frame thy fearful symmetry?

First, students thought that this was a "pastoral" world, with tree, green grass, and a lamblike tyger. Then someone noticed

From William Blake's *Songs of Innocence and of Experience,* edited by Geoffrey Keynes, 1967; reprint, New York: Orion, 1971, plate 42.

55

that the tree seemed leafless and dead. But after a momentary rejection of "pastoral" (because of the dead tree), someone proposed that *the leaves may simply be flourishing off the page,* out of sight, that one may fantasize the idyll rescuing us from reality even if the idyll is not immediately before us. Hovering above (in a heaven beyond mortal sight) is a rescuer in the form of organic creation (leaves) yet still "framing" the picture and the poem. Both questioning and creating are now blessed by the authenticity of natural, idyllic ease. How powerful is the need to be rescued, by an unknown rescuer, from the implications of questioning!

The proposal that the idyll controlled the movement of mind in the poem extended to a misreading of creativity: the role of the blacksmith (i.e., creator-questioner as laborer) was at first altogether missed, but several students talked readily about creation as "birth" and as the "budding" of flowers. That is, they projected an image of creation as natural, essentially without human will and energy. (The idyllic myth of childbirth, of course, does not require the reality of will and energy!) Trapped in this view of mind and of creativity, they could not easily get past the view of the tyger and the fire in the opening stanza, the view that both are distant, scary, and dangerous.

> Tyger Tyger, burning bright,
> In the forests of the night;
> What immortal hand or eye,
> Could frame thy fearful symmetry?

The students were like the speaker of this stanza, caught in the pleasurable fear of sublime questioning, formulating the presence of a distant awesome creator, capable of awesome acts of power including perhaps the rescue of the self from external terror.

In such a view of holy or unholy power encircling the subject, the act of questioning would precipitate the same emptiness and aimlessness it does for the Creature of Wordsworth's "Ode." But for Blake, power resides in the very act of questioning and therefore in the subject. The world of such a question does not empty out before his cry but rather draws the fullness of the object and also the fullness of his fantasies to his being. Questions make of all existence an energy field. Fire, the image of energy in the poem, cannot be contained by distancing it or contextualizing it, as is what happens to the Creature of the "Ode." The eye, only for an instant, holds the fire, but really the fire is continuous with the tyger. The poem enacts the meaning of giving form, through questions, to energy; in this sense the "answers" to the questions reside in the questions themselves. Everything in the poem affirms the act of questioning as the bond of the human subject with his world. Since this bond is a structure of mind and energy, and since a question describes the limits of knowledge while envisioning possibility beyond those limits, the question becomes the syntax of energy as creation. Finally, and most significantly, the privileged reality is that of ideas; the subordinate reality is the experience of the self as subject.

Fantasies encompass all the stanzas of "The Tyger" but particularly the middle four, all of which are saturated — indeed determined — by mythological and Biblical associations. These fantasies are deeper than the "wandering" freedom of mind proposed by the idyll and less chaste in consciousness, honoring the patterns of unconscious wishes and fears, patterns that acknowledge the dramas recognized by both the family and Western civilization; they are what the poet calls on to register his awe and concern in the presence of the tyger. Speaking fantasy, which we might think would imply the speaker's self-absorption, is the content of his questions, that is, of his extension of himself towards the other subject. That the fantasies refer not only to energy but to rebellion and transgression suggests that in the realm of social documents like poems the basic effort of human connection and empathy can carry a subversive burden. The classic ideology of creativity which we inherit from the late eighteenth century gives way to the view of creativity as human labor (the blacksmith), with its Biblical (visionary) and also its contemporary social-class resonances. The subversive fantasies of creation compress (as they do later in, say, some essays by Hazlitt) aristocratic — i.e., "literary" — and lower-class associations.

As the vision of the creator is slowly created, it merges with its "creature," the tyger, in a way that makes it hard to distinguish between the two and, since he imagines creation so intensely, between these two and the speaker. To whom does the "shoulder" belong—creator or tyger? The anatomy of the tyger, as it comes into being, seems largely to be as well the anatomy of the creator:

> And what shoulder, & what art,
> Could twist the sinews of thy heart?
> And when thy heart began to beat,
> What dread hand? & what dread feet?

Yet they are not one, because the spirit of joy and energy in the object that comes into being is just the opposite of any giving up of self into the object: "And did he smile his work to see?"

(The naming of anatomical parts in the creation of "The Tyger" brings to mind Frankenstein's creation of his monster. Here creation fosters the opposite of empathy—alienation and fear, the separation from the offspring and the separation from divinity. Frankenstein lives out the fearful fantasy of transgression, the fear of murder. He too was a questioner who learned to despise and regret his mind's energy.)

"The Tyger" is at once addressed to and about God. Like the Psalms it hammers out an understanding of God by beseeching his response. Unlike the Psalms it discovers the divine presence in the blaze of the questioner's own questions, which do not—as in Wordsworth—formulate and state the need for rescue. My students were enspirited by this crisis of engagement with the divine and (like many of Blake's receptive readers) rejoiced in the surprises of Blake's associations: what an unexpected freedom of imagination in the presence of a fearsome object! Could this be a choice for one committed to life through religion? Could questioning itself be a source of beauty and a way to it?

7   Imitation and Development

Blake's evocation of imaginative freedom is not the place for spiritual wandering evoked by the students. The idyll of mental leisure, moreover, casts a shadow upon an apparently opposite mental activity described in the "Ode," imitation. Section VII defines childhood as a time of imitation of models of social and ritual life:

> Behold the Child among his new-born blisses,
> A six years' Darling of a pigmy size!
> See, where 'mid work of his own hand he lies,
> Fretted by sallies of his mother's kisses,
> With light upon him from his father's eyes!
> See, at his feet, some little plan or chart,
> Some fragment from his dream of human life,
> Shaped by himself with newly-learned art;
>   A wedding or a festival,
>   A mourning or a funeral;
>   And this hath now his heart,
>   And unto this he frames his song:
>   Then will he fit his tongue
> To dialogues of business, love, or strife;
>   But it will not be long
>   Ere this be thrown aside,
>   And with new joy and pride

> The little Actor cons another part;
> Filling from time to time his "humorous stage"
> With all the Persons, down to palsied Age,
> That Life brings with her in her equipage;
>   As if his whole vocation
>   Were endless imitation.

Wordsworth makes imitation difficult for us to evaluate. On the one hand, he places it after two sections which describe, for the growing child, the gradual dilution of divine presence, so that the imitation of adults is a stage in the youth-long falling away from grace. He offers that life here is a play, that all the world's a stage with the child a "little Actor" endlessly conning part after part. The imprisoned child slavishly and mechanically spends his days in this false relationship to life, perverting his birthright and his awesome visionary capacities ("Thou Eye among the blind! Mighty Prophet! Seer blest!"), and forcing the poet into his grandest and most tragic questioning:

> Why with such earnest pains dost thou provoke
> The years to bring the inevitable yoke,
> Thus blindly with thy blessedness at strife?

Section VII opens with the young child surrounded by parental love and hope. Yet in the context these parents, like the foster-mother Earth of the preceding section, reinforce the imprisoning conspiracy; their love does not nurture and embolden but rather lures the child into this complacent imitation. Implicit in these odd resonances in family love is the belief in the demand of the creative imagination for solitude and singleness. A child of God is not really a child. Throughout sections VII and VIII the epithets for the child omit childhood: Actor, Philosopher, Prophet. When he is finally called "little Child," it is only to register the perversity of his behavior. Indeed, childhood in these sections seems perverse, just as does imitation: fallen, evil, and perhaps illusory.

At the same time a tone of exuberance and energy pervades these descriptions: undeniably the child loves to imitate: "this *hath now his heart,*" "with new joy and pride." And if one disregards the context, the parents are seen as only successfully fostering this exuberance. Modern psychoanalytic, as well as Piagetian, thinking regard imitation as an essential activity for the child trying to get a grip on its world: the child imitates others in order to know and act in the world and begins by mimicking those close by, its parents.

Why does Wordsworth insist upon both positive and negative readings? Is it his own ambivalence about imitation? Perhaps, but more relevant to the students' response is to see this as a manipulation of the reader's evaluation of the moment, the demand that he not be able to settle the matter of imitation, or rather that he not be able to feel that he has settled it. For one would have to say that imitation is ultimately seen as a symptom of the fallen state; the sympathy given to the "little Actor" therefore stands isolated from the final evaluation of him, creating a longing for imitation as a valued and effectual activity. We further long for the belief that we are inspired by others, that our acts of imitation are acts of love. Out of this desire we learn, through the poem, to accept the view that the solitude that cultivates and recalls our divine origins is to be preferred.

Imitation is a risk taking. The child, by identifying with a parent, according to Freud at least, wishes to imitate the parent's desire for the heterosexual partner — a desire from which he must be rebuffed. Imitation encourages fantasies of desire and aggression. In the "Ode" the Oedipal fantasy colors the view of the imitating child and may explain the protest, in section VIII, against the child's instincts. The isolated, bewildered, questioning child who then appears in the poem is the grim consequence of the innocent imitator.

But should this have to be? The imitative impulse belongs to the deepest, most archaic levels of the self. A passage from Walter Benjamin recalls, and could be said to interpret, Wordsworth's "Ode":

> We must assume in principle that in the remote past the processes considered imitable included those in the sky. In dance,

on other cultic occasions, such imitation could be produced, such similarity manipulated. But if the mimetic genius was really a life-determining force for the ancients, it is not difficult to imagine that the newborn child was thought to be in full possession of this gift, and in particular to be perfectly molded on the structure of cosmic being.[1]

Imitation could be the child's link to the cosmos, to the sources of life, not his separation from them. He imitates, after all, those ritual moments that in themselves acknowledge the beginnings and endings and eternal repetitions which even in the modern world have not lost their power. Benjamin speculates that the decay of imitation since the time of the ancients with their "magical correspondences and analogies" can be reversed or transformed through language. In particular, written language, containing too the unconscious wishes of the writer, "does not develop in isolation from its other, semiotic aspect. Rather, the mimetic element in language can, like a flame, manifest itself only through a kind of bearer. This bearer is the semiotic element. Thus the coherence of words or sentences is the bearer through which, like a flash, similarity appears."[2] Translated into Wordsworth's "Ode," this would suggest that the imitating child and the questioning one are compatible, and that the primitivism in imitation as magical animation is one with imitation as socialization. Yet Wordsworth refuses this compatibility: imitation and questioning are at odds with each other, which may explain the terrible loneliness and distortion of the questioner (section IX).

One day the following sentence startled me in a student's notebook: "I feel that if I knew how to write, the poem might have been my own." Recognizing the tiresome and familiar disclaimer to thought, "I feel that," and the abdication of the subject of the dependent clause in the independent one does not erase the strange power of the sentence. Indeed, I do not think the sentiment could have been conveyed more accurately. We expect the sentence to

---

1. Walter Benjamin, *Reflections* (New York: Harcourt Brace Jovanovich, 1978), 334.
2. Ibid.

go: "I feel that if I knew how to write, I would have written the poem." We expect him, from the dependent clause, to refer to the activity of writing; instead the activity seems elided or suspended in the apparently more commanding presence of the object, the already existing thing. The student, I think, is caught between the assumption that poetry is created by an original genius, *ab nihilo,* and an intuition that writing-as-imitation would appropriate it for himself. The power of the "Ode" has suddenly reached him, but just as he feels it, he feels his impotence to get nearer to it by imitation through writing. "I feel that" focuses the intuitive nature of the discovery, a "flash" or "gleam" of connection with power, meaning, and beauty, but for him it feels as though language has long been drained of its imitative capacity, probably because he has learned that the only thing language bears is information. So "I feel that" registers the eruption of a longing to stand free of the dispensations of technological society, the tyrannous myth of original genius, the tyrannous decree that imitation is evil and degraded.

The students and I now had completed our discussion of the text of the "Ode," free from "outside" influence. They had at once experienced Wordsworth's generally consoling intention and learned what it was they were experiencing. Apparently caught in conflicts — about transcendence, questioning, and imitation — similar to those of Wordsworth himself, they could begin to move beyond the experience of literature-as-consolation. Just as the college student occasionally will mourn his or her willed distancing from the familiarity of home and family, so my students could mourn the innocence of their initial response to Wordsworth's power. In this regard, tangled in Wordsworth's own confusions about loss and gain, we thought that perhaps the real "kick" from the poem was delivered in the final section when the poet openly acknowledges, amidst all his self-consciousness, his wish for that archaic, innocent source of joy:

> And O, ye Fountains, Meadows, Hills, and Groves,
> Forbode not any severing of our loves!

Part Three
The History of the Ode

8   Horace

So far, in the course, the students had held only the poem before them for their scrutiny, and they had been asked to make a simple set of interrelated observations. (1) The speaker of the "Ode" prefers a realm of inner states leading him to (2) reject or not acknowledge the obvious forms of external reality. This reality includes (3) the implications of questions, namely, the otherness of answers and the speaker's acceptance of his social (human) community, and (4) the implications of imitation, which leads the child into our world partly through his creation of it. The ambivalence toward questioning and imitation comes about as the need strengthens for an external force to rescue him from reality and preserve the self in a supposedly original integrity. For the students, these observations fostered criticism but also acceptance. At this point, I would have to say, acceptance weighed heavier in the balance. When they then turned to the study of the history of the ode, they had to confront on a general level these same observations, but specifically how they related to the myths of the poetic composition. The history of a genre reveals the strong poet not in solitary, divine, original inspiration, but in, as Bloom has argued, an unending struggle with precursor models. The poetic "self" is in this sense under stress, *questioning* the capacity of earlier models to fit his own conception of and confrontation with reality and creating anew by *imitating* the models, asserting and yet transgressing their authority.

I have never been very successful at teaching genre to beginning (or for that matter to advanced) students. This course helped
me to understand why: most presentations of genre in English
departments assume that genre is an aversive fact of literary studies
to be known for examinations but that has relatively little to do
with the "meaning" of a work. A genre is a vessel for what needs
communication, but itself communicates nothing. That it might
be a point of view, have its own politics or metaphysics with which
the poet must contend is not usually considered in the classroom.
But mostly the neglect of the power and necessity of genre comes
from the tendency to organize courses as surveys: one pays so
many dollars per course and ought to receive a reasonable number of goods in return. Even in the intensive study of one author,
one intends to get the biggest survey of his or her works as possible. The author's struggle with genre rarely appears as an authentic fact of the history of composition, and the work rarely
appears as a restless birth in a family of constantly shifting and
mutually determining relations. In our study of the history of
the western ode from Pindar to Keats, the class inserted Wordsworth's "Ode" as one side of a dialogue, the other side of which
was the other ode then in the discussion. The "Ode" began to
lose its pure objecthood and, subjectively, to lose the loneliness
projected upon it by students. It also lost some of the "aura" surrounding it and its author; it became more of an artifact and
less an object sent from eternity. While it could be described solely
in terms of generic properties and thus simplified, it demanded
a more intense and critical use of mind to begin to answer the
questions which the history of genre raised. This stage of the
discussion launched a process which only the end of the term
brought to a close — the experience of the poem as a social and
political occasion. I mean this in two ways: the poem as artifact
could most richly be encountered in the livingness of its histories;
the poem occasioned in the class a discussion the fullness of which
depended upon individuals' varying responses to the challenges
to received opinion raised in historical interpretations.

What follows, in this and the next two chapers, is not that
discussion but a kind of critical set piece from which the class-

room discussion about the history of the "Ode" emerged. It is basically a digression from the dialogic format of this book.

In presenting the tradition of the ode, I attempted first to instruct in the nature of poetry itself, so that the "Ode" was a subset of all — or at least a strong line of — poems. The fundamentally social and political fact of poetry had been impressed upon me in the teaching and writing of my former teacher at Brandeis University, Allen Grossman. His view, that poetry seeks to conserve the image of the hero across time, has always seemed to me very compelling and moving. In that view we are all subject to the denial of access to the community, all falling away from its nurturance; the poem represents the fundamental counterstatement to oblivion and isolation. It represents commitment to the acknowledgment of the person by the community of civilization. Many students (not necessarily the best) communicate that they are already forgotten, that they are without the power to sustain themselves effectually in the presence of another individual. The issue is not precisely immortality, but presence. The attraction of fundamentalism is that it may be seen as a technology of presence, in which the appropriation of the authoritative language of the New Testament seems to serve as presence for those who do not trust it in themselves. That poetry proves an instance of human effort to conserve and therefore to assert such presence appeared to many students as a welcoming possibility. Forgetfulness or oblivion has been seen as a major problem for the poet since Homer, but since the holocausts — real and as yet projected — of the twentieth century it has become even more of a barrier to the consciousness of the person as a member of a community, and particularly of a community that includes all social classes. It is to the process of restoring persons to a community continually being eroded by its members that I address the issue of poetry.

For my purposes, therefore, the *locus classicus* of the ode was Horace, book 4, ode 9, *In praise of the magistrate Lollius:*

> Ne forte credas interitura quae
> longe sonantem natus ad Aufidum

non ante vulgatas per artes
   verba loquor socianda chordis:

non, si priores Maeonius tenet
sedes Homerus, Pindaricae latent
   Ceaeque et Alcaei minaces
      Stesichorique graves Camenae;

nec siquid olim lusit Anacreon
delevit aetas; spirat adhuc amor
   vivuntque commissi calores
      Aeoliae fidibus puellae.

non sola comptos arsit adulteri
crines et aurum vestibus illitum
   mirata regalesque cultus
      et comites Helene Lacaena,

primusve Teucer tela Cydonio
direxit arcu; non semel Ilios
   vexata; non pugnavit ingens
      Idomeneus Sthenelusve solus

dicenda Musis proelia; non ferox
Hector vel acer Deiphobus graves
   excepit ictus pro pudicis
      coniugibus puerisque primus.

Vixere fortes ante Agememnona
multi; sed omnes inlacrimabiles
   urgentur ignotique longa
      nocte, carent quia vate sacro.

paulum sepultae distat inertiae
celata virtus. non ego te meis
   chartis inornatum silebo,
      totve tuos patiar labores

impune, Lolli, carpere lividas
obliviones. est animus tibi
   rerumque prudens et secundis
      temporibus dubiisque rectus,

vindex avarae fraudis et abstinens
ducentis ad se cuncta pecuniae,
    consulque non unius anni,
        sed quotiens bonus atque fidus

iudex honestrum praetulit utili,
reiecit alto dona nocentium
    vultu, per obstantes catervas
        explicuit sua victor arma.

non possidentem multa vocaveris
recte beatum; rectius occupat
    nomen beati, qui deorum
        muneribus sapienter uti

duramque callet pauperiem pati
peiusque leto flagitium timet,
    non ille procaris amicis
        aut patria timidus perire

[Think not the words will perish which I, born near far-sounding Aufidus, utter for linking with the lyre, by arts not hitherto revealed! E'en though Maeonian Homer holds the place of honour, yet Pindar's Muse is not unknown, or that of Ceos, of threatening Alcaeus, or of Stesichorus the stately. Nor has time destroyed whate'er Anacreon once sung in sport. Still breathes the love of the Aeolian maid, and lives her passion confided to the lyre.

Not Spartan Helen only became inflamed with love, marvelling at a paramour's trim locks, his gold-bespangled raiment, his princely pomp and followers; nor was Teucer first to speed the shaft from Cretan bow. Not once alone has an Ilium been beset; nor has great Idomeneus or Sthenelus alone fought battles worthy to be sung by the Muses. Nor were doughty Hector and keen Deiphobus the first to encounter heavy blows for chaste wife and children. Many heroes lived before Agamemnon; but all are overwhelmed in unending night, unwept, unknown, because they lack a sacred bard. In the tomb, hidden worth differs little from cowardice. Not thee, O Lollius, will I leave unsung, unhonoured by my verse; nor will I suffer envious forgetfulness to prey undisturbed upon thy many exploits. A mind thou hast, experienced in affairs, well-poised in weal or woe, punishing greedy fraud, holding aloof from money that draws all things to itself, thou a consul not of a single year, but so oft as, a judge righteous and true, thou preferrest honour to expediency, rejectest with high disdain the bribes of guilty men, and bearest thine arms victorious through opposing hosts.

Not him who possesses much, would one rightly call the happy man; he more fitly gains that name who knows how to use with wisdom the blessings of the gods, to endure hard poverty, and who fears dishonour worse than death, not afraid to die for cherished friends or fatherland.][1]

This very beautiful poem manages the double crisis of the poet's own presence and that of his subject. Horace defines his own activity in terms of three generations of poets, not historically contiguous but following one upon the other in the necessarily changing demands placed on the poet as one whose task is to confer immortality upon his subject. Correspondingly there are three generations of heroes: Homer and the heroes of the Trojan war, the next generation of lyric poets and their heroes of love and war, and himself and his civic hero Lollius. It is easy to describe the poet's concern in the language of "belatedness," the anxiety of influence, the fear of having nothing to say, being invisible before the unbending authority of Homer. The drama of "genre" leaps out of this poem simultaneously with the drama of conserving the image of the hero Lollius, while the poet seems by the way forced to "publish" (*per vulgatas artes*) the intimate thought of his own vulnerability to oblivion; he is drawn visibly into the crisis of conferring visibility upon another. Horace's consciousness of the rigors of genre fills the task of serving his community with praise of its hero. Why does the poet need to take this burdened, self-conscious route to his intended aim of praise? The modern assumptions of originality, spontaneity, and freedom in the creative act are unknown to Horace.

1. Horace, *The Odes and Epodes,* Loeb Classical Library edition, trans. C. E. Bennett (Cambridge: Harvard University Press, 1960), 318–23.

What specifically in form and theme challenge him? He answers the authority of epic form by citing the fact of conveying the image of the person in the slighter forms which approximate his own. But the biggest problem is in the nature of what is to be conserved. Homer's heroes and heroines are all aristocrats. His and the others' heroes achieved their worthiness in battle, love, and the games. Physical passion, *calores,* and strength enspirit their greatness. Praise of Lollius means bestowing heroic stature upon new attributes, those of a governor: judiciousness, hatred of monied interest, honesty, the power and intelligence and tact of a military commander, endurance, lived patriotism. Energy must be employed in a resistance to, not an expression of, impulse: his *animus* must not be *ferox* and *acer* but *prudens* and *rectus.* The poet not only conserves the image of the hero but redefines the hero at the same time.

He also defines and redefines the task of the poet and heroically places himself at the center of the process of redefinition, not in a self-aggrandizing spirit but for the sake of emphasizing the indispensable function of the poet for increasing the happiness and dignity of the person hungering for a meaningful home in his civilization. Inevitably students seem embarrassed by a poet's inclusion of himself in greatness (they find Dante's assertion of his future immortality among the great poets also embarrassing) largely because they see such an assertion as an acquisition standing separate from the momentousness of the task of the poet; they see it as vulgar, as if the poet were predicting that he would end his days a millionaire. They do not consider it a trial composed of conscious humility, daring and — not the least of it — skill.

> vixere fortes ante Agamemnona,
> multi, sed omnes inlacrimabiles
>   urgentur ignotique longa
>   nocte, carent quia vate sacro.

> [Many heroes lived before Agamemnon; but all are overwhelmed in unending night, unwept, unknown, because they lack a sacred bard.]

This stanza sums up a cosmic pathos to which the poem has repeatedly referred: the scarcity of lives granted representation and therefore continuity and immortality, the multitudes of those energetic, effectual heroes (*fortes*) whose lives are denied access to our community because they have been forgotten. That oblivion should make us suffer in the loneliness their vanishing has conferred upon us. For Horace we are stifled because without their image we cannot grieve for them. Could the communal significance of elegy be expressed more touchingly? Could we be invited to understand more simply what makes the bard sacred?

The poet confers immortality on the hero (and by extension on us) not only by restoring his image but also by establishing the values by which heroism is to be measured. There are preferences for the way our energies are to be deployed, preferences not fundamentally "eternal" but culled from the needs and conditions of the contemporary civilization. Yet having realized this, we must also become aware in what way Horace's argument for us masks the historical reality of Lollius. By situating his act of praise in the grand, dignified tradition of poets, he makes us forget to ask: who was Lollius? and who or what was Lollius to Horace? He was, first of all, a *novus homo,* a man emerging out of the nonaristocratic class to enter public politics, someone not born into public visibility, a fact that immediately distinguishes him from the assumed aristocracy of the Homeric hero. He is someone who, in poetry, did not yet in this sense have an image to be praised. "In the tomb," writes the translator, "hidden worth differs little from cowardice." But *inertia* means only secondarily "cowardice," or as it is elsewhere translated, "disgrace"; primarily it means "inactivity." Those outside the public sphere do not act. Lollius, not granted dignity by birth, has chosen activity.

Activity itself, however, is not enough, for Lollius' actions were not universally approved. There were rumors of corruption and deviousness, of precisely the kind of avaricious ambition that Horace said he disdained. If Horace, loyal to his friend and patron, the Emperor Augustus, promoted Lollius' value to the state, the historian Velleius, blindly loyal to the next emperor Tiberius, found Lollius despicable. The name of Lollius, in other words, meant controversy. He was not without an image, but that image looked different to different people depending on their own loyalties, beliefs, and prejudices. We can see a political motive in Horace's urgency in placing him beyond politics. The poet, by invoking the definitions of poetry and marshalling the power of genre, exploits the compelling possibilities of transcendence, permanence, and community as a response to political entanglement. He does, however, refuse to burden with this entanglement either his hero, the genre, or his self-representation. Perhaps his contemporaries chose to read the poem with the appropriate political consciousness. But for us the historical *inertia* requires more of an heroic counterforce. The knowledge of Lollius destabilizes our embrace of this poem; we are still moved but are forced into a particular discomfort. Yet we also know that the ode traditionally has the public in view. When we resist the consequences of this tradition, we evade its essential nature. Less moralistically, we experience the tenacity of the modern ideology of poetry.

9   The Ode Tradition through Collins

A touchstone throughout later discussions of the "Ode," Horace's poem brought the class to some of the characteristics of the ode and some of the responsibilities required of them in the reading of Wordsworth: (1) that most odes project a personal voice stretching beyond itself to some sense of the community or of the public; (2) that the ode praises or celebrates a hero; (3) that it contemporizes the constitution of the heroic; (4) that to confer visibility upon the hero is to give him access to the "community of civilization"; and (5) that for the student to identify with the rhetoric of celebration does not fully give recognition to various kinds of available history.

Reading eighteenth-century odes by Gray and Collins, after reading classical and Renaissance odes, let the students observe the decisive shifts in the more recent thinking about the hero or person celebrated and therefore about decisive shifts in value and human possibility. The key lies in the new concept of the self. The self stands separate from and often antagonistic to society, most intact when least influenced or contaminated by "worldly" matters and relations. The poet praises human types on the periphery of society, such as Horace's *beatus ille*—in its puffed-up eighteenth-century form—retired from commerce to nature. He praises the innocent child, valued—unlike the traditional hero—not for what he does but for what he *is*. Eighteenth-

century writers note again and again the basic connection between the social and political passions and the erotic ones. The
figure of retirement, it follows, is chaste — in every sense, just
as contemplation itself in this context becomes chaste. This self
becomes more "democratic" in the sense that everyone is pur-
ported to have a "soul." Yet, bewilderingly, this democratic community is made up of persons claiming the self-enhancement from
solitude.

After Horace they first read a fragment of Pindar's Ninth Isth-
mian Ode:

> Glorious is the legend of Aiakos, glorious the fame by sea of
>   Aigina. By the gods' good will
> the Dorian host of Hyllos
> and Aigimios, there arriving,
> founded her; by their standards administered
> her people live, transgressing
> no right nor privilege of strangers; for active achievement
> they are dolphins in the sea: accomplished dispensers
> of the Muses, and the games' endeavors.[1]

This extant fragment allowed attention to fall upon the poet's
preference for celebration of the city of which the athletic hero
was a manifestation — the city as the visible results of a history
and as the source of certain kinds of prowess. Also, the ode celebrated not a *being* but an act, an exertion of skill and will. Then
they read Horace's *carpe diem* ode, book 1, ode XI:

> Tu ne quaesieris — scire nefas — quem mihi, quem tibi
> finem di dederint, Leuconoe, nec Babylonios
> temptaris numeros. ut melius, quicquid erit, pati:
> seu plures hiemes, seu tribuit Iuppiter ultimam,
> quae nunc oppositis debilitat pumicibus mare
> Tyrrhenum. sapias, vina liques, et spatio brevi
> spem longam reseces. dum loquimur, fugerit invida
> aetas: carpe diem, quam minimum credula postero.

---

1. Richmond Lattimore, trans., *Greek Lyrics* (Chicago: University of Chicago Press, 1970), 57.

[Ask not, Leuconoe (we cannot know), what end the gods have set for me, for thee, nor make trial of the Babylonian tables! How much better to endure whatever comes, whether Jupiter allots us added winters or whether this is last, which now wears out the Tuscan Sea upon the barrier of the cliffs! Show wisdom. Strain clear the wine; and since life is brief, cut short far-reaching hopes! Even while we speak, envious Time has sped. Reap the harvest of to-day, putting as little trust as may be in the morrow!][2]

Here we discussed the ode's predisposition for general statement, the aphorism, the inclination for the "eternally true."

Before leaving the odes of the ancient world, the students read Horace's *Epode 2,* a poem offering an alternative to the image of the person-as-citizen; here it is the person-in-retirement. The poem begins:

"Beatus ille qui procul negotiis,
    ut prisca gens mortalium,
paterna rura bobus exercet suis
    solutus omni faenore,
. . . .

libet iacere modo sub antique ilice,
    modo in tenaci gramine.
labuntur altis interim ripis aquae,
    queruntur in silvis aves,
fontesque lymphis obstrepunt manantibus,
    somnos quod invitet leves."

["Happy the man who, far away from business cares, like the pristine race of mortals, works his ancestral acres with his steers, from all money-lending free. . . .'Tis pleasant, now to lie beneath some ancient ilex-tree, now on the matted turf. Meanwhile the rills glide between their high banks; birds warble in the woods; the fountains plash with their flowing water, a sound to invite soft slumbers."][3]

---

2. Horace, *Odes and Epodes,* Loeb Classical Library edition, trans. C. E. Bennett (Cambridge: Harvard University Press, 1960), 32–33.
   3. Ibid., 364–67.

Horace associates retirement with a time before the polis, an age golden because society and commercial exchange do not yet exist; in retirement the person abandons the upright community of citizens for the reclining (*iacere*) and pleasurable "society" of nature which leads to the willed abandonment of mind and consciousness (*somnos invitet leves*) for pleasant oblivion. The end of the poem, however, emphasizes the vacation mood of the speaker and his tie to his obsession with money lending; permanent retirement is a fantasy allowed by his commitment to commerce. Thus this poem about retirement from public and commercial life still presents the identity of the speaker in relation to and in terms of the life he has supposedly abandoned.

From the English Renaissance the students read Ben Jonson's "Ode to Himself," which bitterly and wittily accuses the public of rejecting his plays and thereby refusing to see the truth about themselves. Like Horace in the Lollius ode, Jonson predicates his choice of genre (the ode) on the rejection of another (the drama) and for similar reasons: drama is no longer a genre adequate for his new purposes. Whereas Horace needed a nonepic form to contain a nonepic hero, and whereas he needed the more personal lyric form to project his reflexive engagement in his new activity, Jonson takes the same revisionary position for more obviously polemical reasons. The poet's anger and bitterness, his irritation, the condemnations of the public, in short his appearance as chief actor in the representation, all make the poem appear a self-preoccupation, a view which of course the title encourages. Moreover, the self of the poem is alienated from society, a fact which raises the question of whether or not the genre of the ode — in which Pindar and Horace praise and align themselves with the establishment by praising the hero—can tolerate an angry, alienated poet. But Jonson brilliantly resolves his problem by associating his alienation with his identification with his former genre, the drama. By claiming that he will now write odes, he enters the formal requirements of praise and establishment support:

> Leave things so prostitute,
> And take the Alcaic lute;

Or thine own Horace, or Anacreon's lyre;
    Warm thee by Pindar's fire:
And though thy nerves be shrunk and blood be cold,
    Ere years have made thee old,
  Strike that disdainful heat
  Throughout, to their defeat:
As curious fools, and envious of thy strain,
May blushing swear, no palsy's in thy brain.
    But when they hear thee sing
    The glories of thy king;
His zeal to God, and his just awe of men,
    They may be bloodshaken, then
Feel such a flesh-quake to possess their powers,
    That no tuned harp like ours,
    In sound of peace or wars,
    Shall truly hit the stars
When they shall read the acts of Charles his reign,
And see his chariot triumph 'bove his wain.

Thus the proposed celebration of the king allows the poet to ful-fill a Horatian principle (to praise someone other than oneself), to return to the fold of the tradition while transforming it. It is at once a literary and a political return.

At first Milton's beautiful odelike poems, "On the Morning of Christ's Nativity" (which the speaker informally labels "my humble ode") and "Lycidas," appear to scatter the public-centeredness of the ode into other concerns and nonheroic types: an infant is the hero of the first poem and an immature poet that of the sec-ond. Christian eternity and heaven, and not the polis, define the terms of value. But true to the ode tradition, these poems only modify the current expectations. Horace, after all, redefined the values worthy of celebration and, accordingly, the hero who em-bodied them. Milton's Christianity relies not on the good, or public, works of a citizen but refers quite simply to his salvation through "the dear might of him that walked the waves" ("Lyci-das"). The infant Christ—"heaven descended" ("Christ's Nativ-ity") like Wordsworth's child after him—has, of course, done nothing, but his Nativity—seen through believing Christian eyes

— signals momentous action in the future. The public view has broadened to the cosmic; civic ethics yield to Christian ethics; nature yields to a supernature; history and the historic moment and the historic act yield to eternity and the unchanging soul.

Yet both poems still reveal a vital sense of the social community. Before the return of the golden age, humankind must face up to history; Christ "on the bitter cross / Must redeem our loss." ("Christ's Nativity"). The poet in "Lycidas" has time to complain about the corruption of the Church. In each case the poet must release himself from the tyranny of the pagan view of significance. In each case the Christian view completely vanquishes its outmoded opposition, but the poet pays time and history their due. For Milton, the citizen, embodied in his struggling self, never thoroughly vanishes. Indeed, the so-called quiet endings of Milton, particularly that in "Lycidas," recall the apocalyptic vision to the historical present — the birth (not the crucifixion and resurrection) of the saviour, the "tomorrow" and "pastures new" of the uncouth singer in "Lycidas." Thus the elegiac paradigm — death and mourning, resurrection and celebration — works in a complex way, allowing for and encouraging the grief work and the loosening of the old commitments but never fully rejecting or negating them.

Studying Marvell's "Horatian Ode" and Dryden's "Ode to Mrs. Anne Killigrew," the class considered further changes in the definition of the hero and also the roles that become available to the poet. For example, Marvell adheres strictly to the need to celebrate the hero, but he begins to question the values of heroism surrounding Cromwell — a change with reference both to the values of the hero and to the degree of the poet's political complacency. But if the seventeenth-century ode deepens the focus upon the poet-speaker's ambivalence about the hero or upon his feelings as an index of involvement with society, Gray's "Ode on a Distant Prospect of Eton College" questions the entire tradition that had made the ode a vehicle for the celebration of civic virtues. At the same time he invokes the Horatian *beatus ille* tradition. For Gray, however, the poet in retirement does not emerge in Horatian ease; rather retirement is associated with bitterness and with a refusal or disparagement of the social demands of adulthood.

Gray's ode celebrates the spontaneous, carefree life of youth. So much is clear, but the celebration is also a manipulation. Youth, first of all, is not refined into its component parts: infancy, childhood, early and late adolescence. Gray's version may refer to Eton school days, but it could or equally could not fit other times of the first two decades of life. Such a simplification serves well his similarly monochromatic picture of adulthood: bleak, miserable, passion- and shame-ridden, avaricious, constricted. This reduction of the stages of man is commonplace in the eighteenth century; even more commonplace is the reduction of thought to happy and sad, "innocent" and "experienced" categories. The pattern of grandiosity and deflation, bliss and its terrifying absence or loss works its way into poems, dramas, and novels. The pattern serves, it seems to me, three functions: first, to show the crushing effects of "society" upon the innocent "soul" of the individual; second, to organize the success or failure of experience through the category of "health"; and third, to demonstrate that the "fancy" of the child cannot affect the "reality" of adult life, that fancy and reality are by definition at odds with each other, and most of all that fancy is dangerous and deluding. The image of the youth carries this great burden of conviction, and as such it becomes the "victim" (line 52) not only of society and adulthood but also of the poet's ideology.

As one student observed Wordsworth's "Ode" slowly enter the tangled web of history, she began to identify with and be encouraged by that complexity. She was willing to associate the tangle of her own adolescent life with a similar perception of the poem. The pressure of idyllic simplicity in the life of Gray's youth causes a tension with the real life of these adolescents, a tension which I encouraged: "The thoughtless day, the easy night, / The spirits pure, the slumbers light" of the Eton school-boys are not something that an eighteen-year-old college student knows. This disparity helped them recognize that the celebration of youth in Gray is also a peculiar interpetation of it, abstracted from their experience of growing up. With this insight it was possible to

follow the process by which Gray softens the reader's resistance
to assessing youth in such one-dimensional ways:

> Ye distant spires, ye antique towers,
> That crown the watery glade,
> Where grateful Science still adores
> Her Henry's holy shade;
> And ye that from the stately brow
> Of Windsor's heights the expanse below
> Of grove, of lawn, of mead survey,
> Whose turf, whose shade, whose flowers among
> Wanders the hoary Thames along
> His silver-winding way.

> Ah, happy hills, ah, pleasing shade,
> Ah, fields beloved in vain,
> Where once my careless childhood strayed,
> A stranger yet to pain!
> I feel the gales, that from ye blow,
> A momentary bliss bestow,
> As waving fresh their gladsome wing,
> My weary soul they seem to soothe,
> And, redolent of joy and youth,
> To breathe a second spring.

> Say, Father Thames, for thou hast seen
> Full many a sprightly race
> Disporting on thy margent green
> The paths of pleasure trace,
> Who foremost now delight to cleave
> With pliant arm thy glassy wave?
> The captive linnet which enthrall?
> What idle progeny succeed
> To chase the rolling circle's speed,
> Or urge the flying ball?

> While some on earnest business bent
> Their murmuring labours ply
> 'Gainst graver hours, that bring constraint
> To sweeten liberty:
> Some bold adventurers disdain

The limits of their little reign,
And unknown regions dare descry:
Still as they run they look behind,
They hear a voice in every wind,
And snatch a fearful joy.

Gay hope is theirs by fancy fed,
Less pleasing when possessed;
The tear forgot as soon as shed,
The sunshine of the breast:
Theirs buxom health of rosy hue,
Wild wit, invention ever-new,
And lively cheer of vigour born;
The thoughtless day, the easy night,
The spirits pure, the slumbers light,
That fly the approach of morn.

Alas, regardless of their doom,
The little victims play!
No sense have they of ills to come,
Nor care beyond today:
Yet see how all around 'em wait
The ministers of human fate,
And black Misfortune's baleful train!
Ah, show them where in ambush stand
To seize their prey the murtherous band!
Ah, tell them, they are men!

These shall the fury Passions tear,
The vultures of the mind,
Disdainful Anger, pallid Fear,
And Shame that skulks behind;
Or pining Love shall waste their youth,
Or Jealousy with rankling tooth,
That inly gnaws the secret heart,
And Envy wan, and faded Care,
Grim-visaged comfortless Despair,
And Sorrow's piercing dart.

Ambition this shall tempt to rise,
Then whirl the wretch from high,
To bitter Scorn a sacrifice,

And grinning Infamy.
The stings of Falsehood those shall try,
And hard Unkindness' altered eye,
That mocks the tear it forced to flow;
And keen Remorse with blood defiled,
And moody Madness laughing wild
Amid severest woe.

Lo, in the vale of years beneath
A grisly troop are seen,
The painful family of Death,
More hideous than their Queen:
This racks the joints, this fires the veins,
That every labouring sinew strains,
Those in the deeper vitals rage:
Lo, Poverty, to fill the band,
That numbs the soul with icy hand,
And slow-consuming Age.

To each his sufferings: all are men,
Condemned alike to groan;
The tender for another's pain,
The unfeeling for his own.
Yet ah! why should they know their fate?
Since sorrow never comes too late,
And happiness too swiftly flies.
Thought would destroy their paradise.
No more; where ignorance is bliss,
'Tis folly to be wise.[4]

The Greek motto from Menander that opens the poem (translated: "I am a man; a sufficient excuse for being unhappy") pre-
judges the outcome of the story of life described. But this gloomy
sentiment is coupled with the genre picture of Eton from a "pleasing prospect" of both spatial and temporal distance. Easily Gray
establishes the connection between the miserable lot of man and
the nostalgic gaze of the poet for former happier, carefree times.

4. Roger Lonsdale, ed., *The Poems of Gray, Collins and Goldsmith* (London:
Longman, 1976), 56–63.

Nostalgia here emerges from perceptions as generalized outline of distant objects; there is no commitment demanded by confrontation either with the object or the past. Celebrating the haze of distance obscures the misery of one associating himself with something that dismisses the importance of objects. In comparison even with Jonson's "Ode to Himself," Gray's poem refuses any of the important autobiography that produced this poem — the death of his friend Richard West; the quarrel with his friend Horace Walpole; the fall from power, in 1742, of Walpole's father Robert Walpole the Prime Minister; the death of his own father in 1741; and his own financial insecurity. Also, the "prospect" from which he views Eton is the grounds of a summer house on the land of Stoke Poges, where he was staying with an uncle Jonathan Rogers, overlooking the Thames Valley and Eton and Windsor. None of this detail is claimed by the poet; indeed he displaces the idealized feelings of childhood onto objects of place: *happy* hills, *pleasing* shade. Childhood is disengaged from himself: "once my careless childhood strayed." The landscape takes on the burden of the poet's own feelings and is to compensate for the objectless world of the poet's present. All the poet claims is the feeling of the wind blowing from Eton, gales which he invests with a fleeting salutary power, consoling and healing. The wind, like that in Wordsworth's "Ode," links contentment not with the social world but with nature. The "ruach" of prophetic-political inspiration, from the Old Testament prophets to its recovery by Shelley in the "Ode to the West Wind," in Gray and Wordsworth is thoroughly naturalized, reduced from its civic complexity to an intimacy with nature. The fantasy of a past momentarily constrained to heal or fill a barren present creates the space for the subsequent representation of the poet's bitterness.

What made so compelling — in the eighteenth century and still to us — this peculiar combination of life seen as a falling off from edenic happiness and the presentation of this loss denuded of historical and biographical detail? Do we fill the space with our own details, or rather our own fantasies of entitlement and despair? Do we identify with that particularly new feature of Gray's poem — the poet's own nostalgia informing the change from youth to adulthood? We are, I think, asked to sympathize with the feeling of having lost an object, a person, an event. There were, as I have shown, such people and events, but all these are dissipated in "school-time," a vague period unified by the idea of bliss but punctuated, demarcated, simply illumined by no personal details. The poet insists that we sympathize with this simplification of experience, that we sympathize from the comforting distance that is the "pleasing prospect" of the poem itself.

Many writers of the eighteenth century worry over the representation of growing up. As the course progressed, I found that the transition from childhood to adulthood occupied more and more fervent attention: the confusing energies of adolescence hit the students, so to speak, where they lived. The flourishing of passion, as an expression of inner turmoil, the search for intimacy, and the range of idealisms all define adolescence. These adolescent passions often, in the eighteenth century, supply the energy and shape to revolutionary consciousness: the danger anticipated by the adolescent is felt by society at large, trying to maintain and strengthen its totalitarian inclinations. Gray's pessimism about growing up, given without the limiting but liberating presence of autobiographical detail, centers on the cruel, self-destructive effect of passion itself:

> These shall the fury Passions tear,
> The vultures of the mind,
> Disdainful Anger, pallid Fear,
> And Shame that skulks behind;
> Or pining Love shall waste their youth,
> Or Jealousy with rankling tooth,
> That inly gnaws the secret heart,
> And Envy wan, and faded Care,
> Grim-visaged comfortless Despair,
> And Sorrow's piercing dart.
>
> Ambition this shall tempt to rise,
> Then whirl the wretch from high,
> To bitter Scorn a sacrifice,
> And grinning Infamy.

> The stings of Falsehood those shall try,
> And hard Unkindness' altered eye,
> That mocks the tear it forced to flow;
> And keen Remorse with blood defiled,
> And moody Madness laughing wild
> Amid severest woe.

Interestingly, this passage is the most heavily literary in the poem, indeed a literary commonplace of the eighteenth century. Its origin exists in *The Aeneid,* book 6, lines 273–81, listing the miseries of life and mind found at the entrance to Hell, but is modernized in Dryden's *Palamon and Arcite,* Pope's *Windsor Forest,* and most tellingly in Thomson's "Spring" which, like Gray's ode, observes that destructive passions follow youthful innocence:

> . . . the passions all
> Have burst their bounds;
> and Reason, half extinct,
> Or impotent, or else approving, sees
> The foul disorder. Anger storms at large
> Without an equal cause; and fell Revenge
> Supports the falling Rage. Close Envy bites
> With venomed tooth; while weak unmanly fear,
> Full of frail fancies, loosens every power.
> Even love itself is bitterness of soul,
> A pleasing anguish pining at the heart.
> Hope sickens with extravagance; and Grief,
> Of life impatient, into madness swells,
> Or in dead silence wastes the weeping hours.
> These, and a thousand mixt emotions more,
> From ever-changing views of good and ill,
> Formed infinitely various, vex the mind
> With endless storm: whence, deeply rankling, grows
> The partial thought, a listless unconcern,
> Cold, and averting from our neighbour's good;
> The dark disgust and hatred, winding wiles,
> Coward deceit, and ruffian violence.

Rousseau could be said to devote most of his *Emile* to this terror of the developing passions: how can one educate the child into adulthood successfully? by diverting the passions of adolescence from their perversely natural objects, women (or men) and the unfairnesses of society. Sexual desire and social (progressive or radical) consciousness need to be subverted in anticipation of them into the energies required to reinforce the supposedly stable hierarchies of idyllic rural life. *Die Leiden des jungen Werthers* (where *Leiden* might be rendered "fury passions") is the great exemplum for Rousseau's concern: passion, when it seeks its natural object, abuts against idyllic domesticity, defeats itself, but causes widespread tremors of grief, sympathy, and eventually probable dissatisfaction with the status quo. Thomson and Gray give early warnings of and try to ward off the storms of passion, still thirty years away, that will inundate the literature of sex and revolution and the Revolution itself.

The child, or youth, in Gray is the image of the hero, perfect and complete in itself, yet undermined in its perfection by its inevitable fall into passion. Gray looks on him with nostalgia and perhaps his own "Envy wan." Not only an image to celebrate, Gray's youth becomes entangled in the poet's own disappointments and competitive strivings, not — in the poem — in a strictly autobiographical way, but by means of the emerging ideology of the bourgeois idyll. My students, fully alert to Wordsworth's debt to and massive revision of Gray, want to explore the fate of the child; they have not quite come to see that the real issue is closer to home, the history of the fate of themselves as adolescents.

Unwilling, or as yet not required or allowed by the poem to identify with the speaker's own troubled relationship to past and present (himself biographically, at age twenty-five, caught in a late- or postadolescent gloom caused by the death of his father six months before and that of his friend West even more recently), the students do not usually have the chance to question the poet's final prescription:

> To each his sufferings: all are men,
> Condemned alike to groan;
> The tender for another's pain,
> The unfeeling for his own.

Yet ah! why should they know their fate?
Since sorrow never comes too late,
And happiness too swiftly flies.
Thought would destroy their paradise.
No more; where ignorance is bliss,
'Tis folly to be wise.

This tells us that (*a*) no action or character can distinguish one person from another — uniformity is the basic fact of life; (*b*) sympathy, that going out of our own nature that Keats and Shelley claim as the great human virtue and effect of great poetry, is undermined by the blanketing of human experience by suffering; and (*c*) because (*a*) and (*b*) are true, the only happiness is ignorance and knowledge only confirms misery. In this formulation knowledge is ineffectual and, since the desire to know comes unbidden with human life, it is not associated with a willed, shaping power to refocus the outcome of one's life. Knowledge and passion are bound to the same wheel of misery; nowhere can they unite in a vision of possibility; nowhere do they serve the individual in his quest for personal happiness and the enlightenment of his society. Although the general sentiment of this passage goes back as far as Sophocles ("of woes thou knowest naught, for ignorance is life's extremest bliss," *Ajax,* lines 554–55), the preference for ignorance, the abandonment of the pursuit of knowledge, evolving into what John Sitter has called the eighteenth-century poet's "flight from history," recurs at many points in eighteenth-century and Romantic poetry and often at moments suggestive of the adolescent individuating, idealizing, or rebelling (with Oedipal resonances of the exploration of the primally forbidden). This poetry often values the halt of powerful adolescent quests and therefore encourages psychological denial or sublimation and political conservatism. The poem that upholds these views becomes a sacred object, consoling the person on behalf of the status quo and apparently rescuing him from his suffering by including him in that community of those "Condemned alike to groan," a (self-contradictory) community of isolated persons. The possibility of this immobile collectivity becomes the rescue fantasy of the adolescent. The thematic con-

cerns of Gray's ode, therefore, converge upon the formal redefinition of the ode itself. It is easy to see that Wordsworth considered the Eton College Ode as a major challenge to the form
and themes of his own "Ode."

Collins' "Ode to Evening" encourages most of the fantasies (including rescue fantasies) that students have about poetry and "the
poet." It is at once seemingly impenetrable and yet desirable; the
speaker is a contemplative who encourages contemplation and
solitude; the relationship between the poet and Evening (a chaste
female muse) seems secretive and forbidden. The density of al-
lusive and "poetic" language, the extravagant and bewildering
opening dependent clause, concretize the desire to know and
possess something precious and dear. When, moreover, one tries
to classify the poem according to the poetic principle of conserving the image of a hero or person other than the poet-speaker,
he encounters a problem — emergent in Gray but far more compelling here — of the stability of that image. Specifically, the fate
of the poet as the image to be conserved is inescapable, and that
image hints at the possibility of self-abandonment simultaneous
with its conservation by the poem. The poem sacralizes the rescue fantasy of — in the words of the great eighteenth-century adolescent Werther — "chaste passion," or passion without consequence. This is the passion, or passive domination, of Odysseus
before the Sirens:

> If aught of oaten stop or pastoral song
> May hope, O pensive Eve, to soothe thy brawling ear,
> > Like thy own solemn springs,
> > Thy springs and dying gales,
> O nymph reserved, while now the bright-haired sun
> Sits in yon western tent, whose cloudy skirts,
> > With brede ethereal wove,
> > O'er hang his wavy bed;
> Now air is hushed, save where the weak-eyed bat
> With short shrill shriek flits by on leathern wing,
> > Or where the beetle winds
> > His small but sullen horn,
> As oft he rises midst the twilight path,
> Against the pilgrim borne in heedless hum:

Now teach me, maid composed,
    To breathe some softened strain,
Whose numbers stealing through thy darkening vale
May not unseemly with its stillness suit;
        As musing slow, I hail
        Thy genial loved return!
For when thy folding star arising shows
His paly circlet, at his warning lamp
        The fragrant Hours, and elves
        Who slept in buds the day,
And many a nymph who wreathes her brow with sedge,
And sheds the freshening dew, and, lovelier still,
        The Pensive Pleasures sweet,
        Prepare thy shadowy car.
Then let me rove some wild and heathy Scene,
Or find some Ruin 'midst its dreary Dells,
        Whose Walls more awful nod
        By thy religious Gleams.
But when chill blustering winds or driving rain
Prevent my willing feet, be mine the hut
        That from the mountain's side
        Views wilds and swelling floods,
And hamlets brown, and dim-discovered spires,
And hears their simple bell, and marks o'er all
        Thy dewy fingers draw
        The gradual dusky veil.
While Spring shall pour his showers, as oft he wont,
And bathe thy breathing tresses, meekest Eve!
        While Summer loves to sport
        Beneath thy lingering light;
While sallow Autumn fills thy lap with leaves,
Or Winter, yelling through the troublous air,
        Affrights thy shrinking train,
        And rudely rends thy robes;
So long, sure-found beneath the sylvan shed,
Shall Fancy, Friendship, Science, smiling *Peace,*
        Thy gentlest influence own,
        And love thy favourite name![5]

5. Ibid., 463–67.

The two primary manifestations of human personality in its freedom are passion and mind, each of which the poetry of the Romantic tradition attempts to subdue before the needs of a society fearful of the individual's freedom. Collins' poem powerfully represents the struggle of the poet to align himself against the individual as a figure who in his freedom can criticize, by his existence and his conscious acts, the repressive world that tries to support or mould him. The struggle first appears in the capitulatory revisions in the 1748 (the above is the 1746) edition of his poems. "Brawling" in line 2 becomes "solemn," thus rendering less contradictory the wish that Evening subdue his voice of critical passion and that "brawling" voice itself: one cannot successfully pray to the chaste goddess in a voice that denies the wish for the subduing of that passion. Similarly the gothic lines 29–32 become:

> Then lead, calm vot'ress, where some sheety lake
> Cheers the lone heath, or some time-hallowed pile
>   Or upland fallows gray
>   Reflect its last cool gleam.

The early version, compared to the later, contradicts the speaker's inclination to give himself up as an agent: instead of roving and finding, he now asks that he *be* led, and calling Eve a "calm vot'ress" insures that he not only give up agency but give up passion as well (a theme of his contemporaries Joseph Warton and Thomas Warton, Sr.). "Calm" is a key word in this and other like poems of the 1740s, indicating the subduing of the passions and (implicit in this) the subduing of critical consciousness. Nature, like the hut that protects the speaker from snow, rain, and wind, becomes a protection from the social world and from the critical thinking that that world can elicit. Typically this poetry contrasts the rural retreat as the locus of the calming of mind and passion to the corrupt passions produced by and in the industrial city (envy, avarice, ambition). But the poets refuse to acknowledge that this position allows them the luxury of not absorbing, as Raymond Williams in *The Country and the City* has convincingly shown, the domination and restriction of laborers in the country. These poets, he speculates, retreat into the melancholy of loneliness and call it freedom of spirit. Nature, traditionally the realm of necessity and mystery, is now to be courted as the place of enlightenment ("Science") and health.

I have already alluded to Odysseus' encounter with the Sirens manifesting the wish for simultaneous self-abandonment and self-preservation. Nature in eighteenth-century poetry charms and enchants like the Sirens but in the poet's commitment to it renders the readers passive (bound to the mast) and ineffectual. By taking on both action and affect (e.g., lines 41–48), Nature becomes a substitute society that, unlike the real one, does not demand that the person confront the painful fact of society, the domination over and repression of the freedom of one or more of its parts by another. The poet is content to live beneath nature's "habitual sway." Yet this submission on his part, of course, masks his own dominant position: like Gray looking down on the "pleasing prospect" of Eton and the past, so Collins hopes to look down upon (dominate, possess with the eye) the hamlets and spires marking civilization, the details of which he keeps from himself by distance and the "dusky veil" of Evening. Self-abandonment (actually displaced onto a lively, creative, at times willed nature) is really less his intent than is self-preservation.

The reader of the poem is invited to assent to its propositions, to let his own wishes flow into the sanctioned current of the poem that will afford protection to and domestication of his own passions. As John Gilbert Cooper wrote in 1755: "The following Scene, in Mr. Collin's Ode to the Evening, being animated by proper Allegorical Personages, and colour'd highly with incidental Expression, warms the breast with a sympathetic Glow of retired Thoughtfulness."[6] What an accurate formulation of the intent of much eighteenth-century and Romantic poetry: the erotization of mind in retirement. To create a poem eliciting sympathy for this state is to seek to create a community (if it can be called that) content with the status quo of domination. The

6. Ibid., 462.

beauty of nature is the charm and enchantment of the Sirens. The nature poet differs from Odysseus first of all in that the latter knows precisely the cost of his self-abandonment (death) and can act to counter the cost (domination of his laboring sailor-slaves). For the nature poet, nature is that which can be possessed, and once possessed it can be embued with therapeutic (animistic) power. The rescue fantasy that is the "Ode to Evening" is finally a fantasy of domination, in which the only residue of the terror of death or dismemberment anticipated by Odysseus is the complacent emotion of melancholy. Perhaps Odysseus' thrill and terror erupted in Collins' life through his self-destructive contortions of bewildering madness.

My students, I believe, are bound (unknowingly and without feeling it) to the same wheel of fire. That is, they read poetry under the category of domination. A poem, thoroughly objectified by institutions, a "pleasing prospect" of language, turns active before their passive desire; it is made mysterious and bewitching yet finally appears to yield up a meaning through analysis. Self-abandonment, almost always for the reader a possibility behind the rhetoric of this poetry, rarely reveals itself as a terror and a thrill. But poetic analysis becomes self-abandonment sanctioned by the domination of the institution. The truth of nature, not permitted to consciousness, forces itself nevertheless upon the student by appearing to grant him the power of enlightenment and mastery. Yet this power is transferable only to other poems and only in the form of poetic analysis; the world has not become more real or alive, because the supposed sympathy only acknowledges a subject subdued to the analytic function. This is the meaning of Wordsworth's assertion that we murder to dissect.

10   Coleridge

After Gray and Collins had been studied in the manner thus described, it was easy to present Coleridge's three odes: "To the Departing Year" (1796), "France" (1798), and "Dejection" (1802). The first two political odes represent the abandonment of radical political engagement for the spiritualized peace of—either religious or natural—solitude. The third manages "unimpassioned grief," not by exploration of its cause or by confronting the present but by displacement of passionate feeling onto nature and onto the projected benign life of another person. In all cases the otherness of another—whether political or personal—is abandoned, as is social passion (Rousseau's *amour propre*).

In December 1818 Coleridge wrote to a friend William Collins:

> Poetry is out of the question. The attempt would only hurry me into that sphere of acute feelings, from which abstruse research, the mother of self-oblivion, presents an asylum.[1]

Written about two decades after the three odes, these sentences —by quoting a vital phrase from "Dejection" ("abstruse research") —still aptly comment on Coleridge's general abandonment of

1. Samuel Taylor Coleridge, *Collected Letters,* ed. Earl Leslie Griggs (Oxford: Clarendon, 1959), 4:893.

poetry and also may explain the challenge, the fear, and the defenses brought to bear against the very nature of poetry while practicing it:

> For not to think of what I needs must feel,
> But to be still and patient, all I can;
> And haply by abstruse research to steal
> From my own nature all the natural man —
> This was my sole resource, my only plan:

Abstruse research (metaphysics? theology?) is a defense against "nature" or passion; earlier he refers to his "unimpassioned grief" "without a pang." But the desired restoration from nature never comes. Instead he turns from his "viper thoughts" to the natural world, displacing his passions onto the "raving" wind and the lute's "scream of agony." It is only a step from this vision of nature's rescue to wishing the "rescue" of the final stanza's "Dear Lady":

> Joy lift her spirit, joy attune her voice;
> To her may all things live, from pole to pole,
> Their life the eddying of her living soul!
> O simple spirit, guided from above,
> Dear Lady! friend devoutest of my choice,
> Thus mayest thou ever, evermore rejoice.

Typically for Coleridge to load another person with celebration, love, and hope means to abandon quite completely affectual self-concentration, so that what at first looks like an "I-Thou" encounter really isn't — instead it's just a projection of a rescue fantasy onto another person. Social passions, it follows, are abandoned too, just as in the earlier political odes the passions of politics are abandoned for idyllic self-involvement and self-preservation. In the "Ode to the Departing Year," entanglement with the vision's revelation of national and international evil is finally dissolved:

> Away, my soul, away!
> I unpartaking of the evil thing,
> With daily prayer and daily toil

> Soliciting for food my scanty soil,
>   Have wail'd my country with a loud Lament.
> Now I recentre my immortal mind
>   In the deep Sabbath of meek self-content;
> Cleans'd from the vaporous passions that bedim
> God's Image, sister of the Seraphim.

Here the recovery of individuality necessitates the abandonment of social activism (which also appears as self-abandonment) and the sublimation of social passion "upward" into religious calm. This movement is dramatized in what have come to signify conventionally Romantic terms in "France: An Ode": the movement from social activist criticism to self-preservation in the natural world. Not wishing to represent this adjustment as an escape or defeat or lapse into passivity, Coleridge effectively transposes the setting, and therefore the meaning, of "Liberty" from the civic and historical (i.e., the French Revolution, criticism of the slave trade) to the natural and the religious:

> With what deep worship have I still adored
> The spirit of divinest Liberty.

Moreover, "Liberty" itself has become its own agent: what once existed in society had "sped" to the natural world. The poet achieves a spiritualization of natural forces which is also a spiritualization of a political ideal:

> Thou speedest on thy subtle pinions,
> The guide of homeless winds, and playmate of the waves!
> And there I felt thee! — on the sea-cliff's verge,
>   Whose pines, scarce travelled by the breeze above,
> Had made one murmur with the distant surge!
> Yes, while I stood and gazed, my temples bare,
> And shot my being through earth, sea, and air,
>   Possessing all things with intensest love,
>   O Liberty! my spirit felt thee there.

What could be seen as an escape from society as the place where the fate of liberty will be decided becomes simply the relocation of liberty. Furthermore liberty is no longer associated with the destabilization of the self in the midst of social struggle. Having deposed the latter from the triangle of self, society, and "liberty," the poet can claim an intimate relationship with liberty. But this, too, smacks of the rescue fantasy: the "guide of homeless winds" becomes the poet's guide, or rather his salvation; and by extension the poem in which this experience is recorded as well as the poet or sacred bard (*vate sacro*), from Horace to Gray (in "The Bard"), validates his interpretation of his experience and seeks to render it impervious to criticism.

Such a solution to the tensions, for adolescents, of the claims of the self and the risks of social consciousness is very appealing because although it does not thwart any latent idealism and activism, it also does not deprive him or her of the instinct for self-preservation in the sacred place of the natural and the beautiful. In this regard Shelley's "Ode to the West Wind" and, to a lesser extent, Keats's odes are at once more threatening and — perhaps on a deeper level, these days, scarcely supportable in the consciousness of most late adolescents — more appealing than the odes of Coleridge since the younger Romantics are readier to commit their identities to their social and sexual passions and drives. Put in terms of the ode's ancient demand for social or civic or philosophic consciousness, the collapse — in the eighteenth century and early Romanticism — of the other into the poet's subjectivity is partly redeemed in Keats and Shelley by the preference in their poetry for passion. And passion, for them, always reflects the recognition of the self's incompleteness and entanglement in the contradiction of society and in the sexual drives. The young people in my course responded noticeably to the sexual and revolutionary underpinnings of the last two stanzas of the "West Wind":

> If I were a dead leaf thou mightest bear:
> If I were a swift cloud to fly with thee;
> A wave to pant beneath thy power, and share
>
> The impulse of thy strength, only less free
> Than thou, O Uncontrollable! If even
> I were as in my boyhood, and could be

The comrade of thy wanderings over Heaven,
As then, when to outstrip thy skiey speed
Scarce seemed a vision; I would ne'er have striven

As thus with thee in prayer in my sore need.
Oh! lift me as a wave, a leaf, a cloud!
I fall upon the thorns of life! I bleed!

A heavy weight of hours has chained and bowed
One too like thee: tameless, and swift, and proud.

V

Make me thy lyre, even as the forest is:
What if my leaves are falling like its own!
The tumult of thy mighty harmonies

Will take from both a deep, autumnal tone,
Sweet though in sadness. Be thou, Spirit fierce,
My spirit! Be thou me, impetuous one!

Drive my dead thoughts over the universe
Like withered leaves to quicken a new birth!
And, by the incantation of this verse,

Scatter, as from an unextinguished hearth
Ashes and sparks, my words among mankind!
Be through my lips to unawakened Earth

The trumpet of a prophecy! O Wind,
If Winter comes, can Spring be far behind?

With difficulty (emotional as well as intellectual) they came to recognize that the poet could not — unlike Coleridge in "France" —
stand easily in the presence of nature and "liberty" because Shelley
finally knows that liberty is partly a function of his own risk in
relation to it. The prayer to the wind for support and transformation is not merely a prayer for rescue. It is a prayer about his own
courage and about the turning of his own poetic language and his
own consciousness of social inequity and oppression toward language as effectual in a revolutionary or reforming sense. The Romantic rhetoric of rescue is thus self-critical here in that Shelley demands more of himself as an historical person and less of nature.

11 Wordsworth's "Ode" in the Ode Tradition

Studying the "Ode" in the history of its genre raised questions not only about the poem's "art" but about ideas and points of view. But even the poem's "art," its so-called formal and aesthetic attributes, turns out also to be embedded in a set of ideas. More specifically, the "beauty" in the "Ode," what it is that makes one assent to the poem, lies largely in a set of ideas congenial to a certain individual in a certain state of mind, an individual wishing to rejoice in a vision of a life of simple coherence and connectedness achieved through an inwardness toward which one might personally strive. Wordsworth saw the form of this ode, and odes written by him ten years later, as traditionally Pindaric (in the eighteenth-century redefinition of a poem wild and irregular in structure and mood); the ideas of the poem mark it as unusual among odes up to Wordsworth's time. Comparing the extravagant changes in the view of the hero, the local interpretations of the public-centeredness of the ode and the relative emphases on the hero as actor versus the hero as one who simply is, the students developed a context for noting and then assessing the idealist values in Wordsworth's "Ode." They became aware of its inwardness and its preference for mind and the mind's transformation of reality over reality itself, its preference for "universal man" over man grounded in historical and psychological particulars. My students had been well trained in this idealist tradition, so that their predisposition led them to find Wordsworth's ideas, as they were realized in the poem, "beautiful." But our continuing study of these ideas in various contexts allowed these young people to criticize and debate these ideas, so that the critical view drew them into conflict with their assent to the poem as beautiful and powerful. The further step remained to show them that Wordsworth and Wordsworth's critics (see chapters 12–16) were not immune to such conflict and that only the idealist/humanist predisposition in their education had led them to see these competing strains in our cultural tradition as nonexistent or at best inconsequential.

I had introduced the students to the section on the ode tradition by showing them the title page to Wordsworth's "Ode" in the first (1807) edition of *Poems* and then in its second (1815) appearance. The early publication simply says "Ode" on one entire page; the second gives the new, elaborate title above the poem: "Ode: Intimations of Immortality from Recollections of Early Childhood." Why, I asked, did Wordsworth alter the title from its radical simplicity to its extravagant complexity? Why did he first call the poem just "Ode," with no "content"? Their initial response, which is partly valid,[1] was that Wordsworth must have decided that the poem needed "clarification"—that is, the first title is "vague." The early reviews of the 1807 volume render the "Ode" nearly invisible or, at best, obscure. The volume as a whole and in its parts received very detailed and committed (though not always positive) response from reviewers. But the "Ode"— given its magisterial size and subject and its prominent positioning as the last poem in the volume—seemed to render reviewers irritable, baffled, or simply speechless. For example, Francis Jeffrey called the "Ode" "beyond all doubt, the most illegible and unintelligible part of the publication [i.e., *Poems, in Two Volumes*]."[2] But this was not the point I wished to make. (Later on we dis-

1. Cf. *The Correspondence of Henry Crabb Robinson with the Wordsworth Circle 1808–1866*, ed. E. J. Morley (Oxford: Clarendon, 1927), 2:838–39.
2. Cf. James Venable Logan, *Wordsworthian Criticism* (Columbus: Ohio State University Press, 1947), 9.

cussed the changes in much greater detail, including in our analysis the change in epigraphs.) I wanted them to see that the title had shifted its emphasis from form to content. Obviously in 1815 Wordsworth, by juxtaposing "Ode" with his strange title, was declaring a new category of subject for the ode, but still the reader's eye falls more heavily upon the subject matter than the form in which it is presented. Far from being "vague" the early title asks the reader specifically to think about form or genre; moreover, it narrows the class of sympathetic readers to that which knows what an ode is — not only its definition but its tradition — and can therefore enter the poem's circuit of power, whether to be unsettled or consoled. To this group of students, in their relative lack of acquaintance with tradition, with its necessity for the artist, and with the whole idea of genre, the plan to launch into a study of the ode tradition came as a surprise; the situation in which they found themselves was new. The survey course is not new or surprising, nor is a course in a genre (e.g., "Development of the English Novel"), but suddenly they found themselves unable to answer a very specific and what looked like simple question which apparently demanded knowledge of the history of a genre. Having studied the poem by way of the history of genre for about a month, they could find the questions I had posed important. The work was no longer "autonomous" and consoling because the possibility existed that it could communicate only through a set of coordinates as yet unknown to them. They could no longer dominate it with their analyses and their beliefs about art as itself the sacred space. Similarly the poem, no longer relegated to eternity, entered history.

Yet immediately after concluding the survey of the ode tradition, some students, instead of seeing Wordsworth's "Ode" brought down to the size of an object in history, once more found it of gigantic proportion. Indeed, perhaps it appeared grander than before, surely more awesome than the odes just studied. I, too, then and now — as I emerge from the week of writing on the odes in the tradition — am swept up by the commanding force of this poem and its vision, the apparently disinterested power of reflection, understanding, and wisdom, the serenity of verbal choice,

the range of musical phrasing. Each section of the poem — unlike
the usual stanza which adds itself bricklike to the structure of
a poem — asserts its own swell and fall, declares its own reality
and vision, like a movement in a noble symphonic or chamber
work. We respond to Wordsworth's transcendence of the tradition.
The poem seems to have reached beyond the public-centeredness,
the very historicity of one strand of the ode tradition, and beyond the particularities of private experience, the subjectivity of
the other strand. It seems to embrace both the formal extravagance of some odes and the formal asceticism of others. It begins and ends in the center of the poet's wavering and emergent
consciousness, yet sets its task for understanding and experience
in the midst of universals. The "terrible questions" at the end
of IV and VIII and the resolution in IX–XI raise the level of
emotion and crisis to a pitch one usually associates with the drama,
perhaps the novel, and, in another medium, music. But if the
substance of Wordsworth's thinking is so compelling, its density
and subtlety are what give the poem its urgency, its authenticity.
Rarely in modern poetry does the speaking self emit such radiance and freedom while it adheres happily to a moral and religious rectitude. The poem, in the context of the ode tradition,
is a divine comedy on the lyrical scale, at once cautious and extravagant, confrontative of terrors and lavish in its deployment
of the consoling, comic framework.

Does one need to go further? Is it not enough to use the tradition to highlight, by contrast if for no other reason, the poem's
greatness? Has not history thus served a noble purpose? Surely
such a discovery imbues the classroom with gratification. The
problem is that the process of mind has not been enhanced. To
end in wonderment is not the point, or it is only part of the point.
The politics of genre studies is usually conservative: since the
work emerges from a tradition, it is forever defined by it, even
if by transcending it. Thus the reader's determination is circu-
lar; the ode is yet an ode even if one exclaims: "*What* an ode!"

So one asks: must such a study of the ode produce the kind
of confirmation of or assent to the ode participant in this tradition? Not, I think, if one makes clear the distinction between

the power of the general (the ode in the tradition) and the power of the particular (Wordsworth's "Ode"). The former cannot be allowed to engulf the latter. In turn, one must define the latter not only by its odelike properties but also by the reader's commitment to experience it in the flux and the coding of its own historical moment. As long as the "Ode" always appears in its relations, it can never completely be defined by the tradition. History in this way gets rehistoricized; the tradition becomes one element in the set of relations. Perhaps this helps us to see why genre studies so often do nothing to detranscendentalize the literary object. They finally refuse to allow the work itself to be defined in its social particularity.

The trajectory of the ode tradition as it reaches Wordsworth's "Ode" we may sum up in terms of the dissolution of the polis — with its insistence upon the recognition of difference among its members — into the Enlightenment utopia of the general equality of selves, or the citizen subsumed by the universal, or essential, "man."

The most important identifying feature of Wordsworth's "Ode" in relation to the tradition is the mind's conversion of reality into its appearance: the citizen becomes the universal "man" (an appearance). Seen in this way the absence or at the very least the obscuring of the Pindaric and Horatian subjects of the Ode — the exemplary citizen to be celebrated — is rationalized in the foregrounding of the poet in the "Ode" by his essential identity with the other. This is comparable to Wordsworth's formula for the poet, "a man speaking to men," in which the speaker and his audience are the same person. By extension, for Wordsworth the speaker, his subject, and his audience are, or must be made to be, identical. When I asked them the fundamental generic question about the "Ode" — whose image does the poet wish to conserve and praise? — the students naturally were confused. They had to figure out how to separate themselves from the poem and the poet from his subject, or — what actually happened — to begin to recognize that Wordsworth had contrived to seal over the distinctions among citizens. This was, of course, particularly difficult since the students' education had led them to wish to lend

themselves to modern cultural anonymity. Many sought the conserved image in the "child" of the poem, celebrated as merely
another manifestation of the flowers and animals early in the poem
and recovered at the end through imagination and metaphor:

> Hence in a season of calm weather
> Though inland far we be,
> Our Souls have sight of that immortal sea
> Which brought us hither,
> Can in a moment travel thither,
> And see the Children sport upon the shore,
> And hear the mighty waters rolling evermore.

It was several weeks later when a student wrote in his notebook
with an appropriate mixture of triumph and exasperation about
the "disquieting" nature of the poem because "the child isn't real,
the heavenly aura isn't real, and the intimations aren't real, but
the emotional content is. . . ."

This young person had managed to verbalize a general lack
of conviction among his peers concerning the image to be celebrated. In contrast to Wordsworth's, Gray's child, though doomed
and weak in its freedom and caught in the poet's own nostalgia,
seemed more recognizable because it retained its distinctness
from the poet. Wordsworth's sophisticated presentation of the role
of imagination, by contrast, converts the absence of persons to
the speaker into apparent presence. No one, of course, actually
believes that children now are where they were not, but the discovery of this power of mind is very seductive. ("We in thought
will join your throng.") For example, Wordsworth brilliantly
brings an elemental vision of the power of the human capacity
for self-preservation through play in the face of a more sinister
power of nature: the children sporting on the shore show the peculiar human resilience in the face of the "mighty waters."[3] "Another race hath been, and other palms are won." The child, then

3. Cf. Wordsworth's acknowledgment of the engulfing power of nature in
The Prelude (1805 edition), book 5, lines 93–139.

(as well as the adult) is endowed with this basic human resilience and is thus worthy of celebration. But that the speaker appropriates childhood to himself through his own imagination weakens the reader's sense of the child's reality just as the poet is making it more vivid. This is what led the student to react to the emptiness of the child in terms of action: one is not real if he does not do something, an observation which implies that the imagination cannot appropriate to itself an independent, or free, subject.

Just as Rousseau, in his *Reveries of the Solitary Walker,* prefers to enjoy what he calls the "spontaneity" of flowers over the spontaneity of social persons, so Wordsworth metaphorizes the living spontaneity of children as social, resilient beings. In each case the imagination fills the absence, or the fear of absence, with its own version of freedom over which, however, it has complete control. Put differently, it creates the illusion of the social situation. (Coleridge, in "Fears in Solitude," goes so far as to refer to the natural world as "society.")

Loss is an important feature of several modern odes — e.g., Gray's Eton College Ode, Coleridge's "France" and "Dejection" odes, and Wordsworth's "Ode." For both Coleridge and Wordsworth loss is tied to the relationship between politics and the imagination. In Horace's Ode to Lollius, however, where the imagination is not an issue, loss refers more fundamentally to the crisis of literary representation itself; the act of conservation of the image of the person makes conscious the inevitability of loss of the person as citizen and the inevitability of grieving for him. Horace calls up an entire civilization that remains forever "unweepable," "illacrimabiles." People who have acted in the world and died, but by definition are unweepable, are the nightmare of the poet who dispels the terror with his own act of representation. When Achilles says to Odysseus in the underworld that he would rather be a slave alive on earth than king of the shades, we do not feel his pain but rather experience relief at discovering him in representation. Surely this same relief is part of the trust Odysseus has in his own craftiness, which is his ability to act both responsibly and daringly in relation to those whose interests lie elsewhere. That is, conservation of the image, or the poet's act in the presence of loss, affirms the tension between the individual and the political community and demands a vision of a person prepared to risk himself.

The eighteenth-century poet is concerned primarily with the opposite of risk: self-preservation. Turning to the subject of loss, he mourns a vanished innocence and freedom, a Heaven, which he often associates with childhood; and just as the mourning of the dead hero preserves, in Max Horkheimer's phrase, "the utopia of eternal happiness,"[4] the latter becomes a possession in poetry even as it has vanished from life. But to possess it in the realm of representation is also to be satisfied that it or some appropriate version cannot be reinitiated in later life; and such a satisfaction signals the decline of the tension between the individual and the political community since the experience of that tension requires the energy of risk in the consciousness of the adolescent or adult. Thus Gray's deploring the loss of childhood does not convince us particularly that it deserves assent or sympathy because in fact he had recovered it in representation. Poetry legitimizes for him his present emptiness by being addressed to a readership itself satisfied with things in society as they are. Coleridge, in "France," makes political belief part of the broken promise of innocent happiness, thereby stating more clearly than most poets the underlying motive of eighteenth-century lyric poetry: the flight from history, seen, however, as an inevitable, biological or geographical, stage in human development. (It is interesting, in this regard, to contrast Coleridge with Milton for whose characters the loss of innocence announced the embrace of history and a future of meaningful action.) Growing up affirms the preference for self-preservation in the bracing solitude of nature over the abandonment to radical political reality. For Wordsworth, politics has been buried deep (although with the study of manuscripts, revisions, and verbal associations to other poems, the

4. Max Horkheimer, "The End of Reason," in *The Essential Frankfurt School Reader*, ed. Andrew Arato and Eike Gebhardt (New York: Urizen Books, 1978), 41.

political origins are revealed). Loss is now transferred to an ineffable state of pre-existence, which, like the poet's moods and perceptions of that state, cannot be proven but must be taken on faith. In addition, if it can be said that the traditional ode attests to the creative tension between the individual and the community and that in Coleridge the tension is felt in the loss of innocence as a developmental stage, then Wordsworth appears to deny the tension through the strange collapse of the idea of development and by the final assertion (again to be taken on faith) that the loss is really no loss at all. The child from whom the "gleam" has fled seems, as my students observed, to be quite without substance and, in section VIII, is addressed in terms that seem to contradict his childlikeness: prophet, seer, philosopher. The loss and recovery, unlike that in "Lycidas" or in "France," employs the basic structure of those poems, but nothing important has been lost. Nor has the poem rendered a conversion to a new perspective and new evaluation of experience, either religious (as in Milton) or naturalistic (as in Coleridge). The "Ode" is completely subjective and is the history and celebration of subjectivity.

Yet Wordsworth's Age, Wordsworth himself, deeply knew the meaning of "citizen" and of "loss." He was living in what Hobsbawm calls the Age of Revolution, even if, as Marilyn Butler has more finely labeled it, the first decade of the nineteenth century was a decade of "counter-revolution." Fully, if temporarily, identified with the social upheavals of his time, Wordsworth could not produce such an idyllic vision of inner struggle without consciously and painstakingly eradicating and altering in the "Ode" the verbal traces of his radical sympathies. The object of the following sections is (and was in the course) to show that in Wordsworth's initial plans for the "Ode" he wished to explore the personal/political tension, but that he carefully and systematically revised this out over the years. Most of these revisions involve the suppression of references to passion, drive, and the senses — all loaded concerns central to late eighteenth-century literary politics. The late eighteenth century often represented rebellion and social criticism in terms of the risks of passion required to effect its goals. In its response to the social constraints on individual freedom imposed by domesticity and institutionalized religion, it spoke in the language and imagery of sexual passion and libidinal and aggressive fantasy. The emphasis in the stages of life falls upon adolescence, where crisis concerns the risks of idealism, the emergence of sexual desire, and the rebellion from paternal authority. For the students, their own crises of adolescence suddenly resonate to the submerged issues of the "Ode."

Part Four
Revision

12   The History of Revision
in the "Ode"

From "Untam'd Pleasure" to "Heaven-born Freedom"

The study of revision, as I said at the beginning, teaches the student that every stage of thought has its own substantive reality and is not merely an imperfect manifestation that will self-destruct before the next, more perfect realization. Every choice of revision is just that, a choice based on the evaluation of the substance and vision of the writing at that moment, and it requires a decision to pursue or alter the vision. At the same time this author making his choice no longer maintains the disinterested perspective; for if he is one who can alter the contents of his writing, he must be considered one who at any given moment has included a bit of what at another moment he would judge inadmissible. Such a judgment does not mean that he is only removing the unnecessary or the superfluous for the sake of concision and clarity, but also that he is shifting the basis on which meaning in the work is to be found. The same reasoning, of course, applies to Wordsworth; what follows is the history of revision of the "Ode" defined in terms of decisions based upon literary/political sympathies.

Take, for example, the momentous 1815 revision of the following lines in the 1807 edition of the "Ode":

> Thou little Child, yet glorious in the might
> Of untam'd pleasures, on thy Being's height,

113

Why with such earnest pains dost thou provoke
The Years to bring the inevitable yoke,
Thus blindly with thy blessedness at strife?

In 1815 Wordsworth altered "untam'd pleasures" to "heaven-born freedom." A slight change, one is ready to say. Yet to take it seriously is to do nothing less than expose to the mind a central issue in the politics of early post-Enlightenment literature and to declare that Wordsworth, far from disinterested, knows the issue and is fully participating in it: how far will one admit to the passional nature of human beings and to what degree will one seek to deny or suppress this nature for the sake of not only the preservation of the individual but also the status quo of patriarchal domination in society? The major writers throughout the second half of the eighteenth century gravitate to this question as if it were one of the very few things worth addressing. The first vision of these lines suggests an elemental "contradiction" in human nature but also points to the answer of Wordsworth's powerful question: the blind striving against one's blessedness is sensuous passion itself, the infinite hunger for life, for relationship, for society, for love, for objects, for knowledge, and the willingness to abandon oneself for the sake of these things. The phrase, "might / Of untam'd pleasures," is at once cast down the long avenue of the classical tradition of the precarious but necessary balance between our "lower" and "higher" selves while it looks forward toward the revolutionary Darwinian and Freudian intimacies with our "animal" nature. Wordsworth seems here to admit to the power, or might, of drives and instinct and pleasure itself and their determining place in the process of growing up. In this he does no more than follow Rousseau in *Emile,* most of which concentrates on the might of the unfolding pleasures and drives of adolescence.

But how does all this square with the supposed "blessedness" of the child? We know by this point in the poem that Wordsworth means to define the child in terms of its sacred, perhaps otherworldly quality. The child is capable of casting over an object a gleam or aura that probably — it is not clear — precludes the need for desire to bring us into relation to every common thing. The fact is that the child of untamed pleasures does not square with the child of blessedness. This does not, however, mean that Wordsworth's first version is not true — if not of human beings, then of a late eighteenth-century fantasy of them. Yet the poet of 1815 chose to deny this contradictory truth for a new consistency in his vision of human life. The contradictory (of a wish for "blessedness" and a recognition of "untam'd pleasures") becomes now a tragedy and a mystery: a tragedy because a child of heaven seems perversely to wish to distance itself from its nature and high origins, a mystery because the reason for this wish is unfathomable. Passion and drive and pleasure, to the degree that they might be posited even when not named, must now be associated with evil or perversity since they would belong to that which leads one away from blessedness. The only acceptable pleasure for the child would be that innocent, pastoral kind in sections III, IV, X, and XI. Pleasure joins in the sacralizing of an idyllic childhood but does not extend into the moment of social consciousness. In 1815 Wordsworth responds to Gray's and Rousseau's gloomy predictions of life after childhood by removing, surgically, the problem, the passions themselves, and replacing them with Heaven as a prosthetic device. The earlier Wordsworth would not evade the contradiction of the age.

But, some still may rightly ask, can one place so much emphasis in a 206-line poem on two or three words? A careful study of all the variants of the poem, from the manuscripts of 1802–4 until the 1836 edition of *Poems* and beyond, shows an unmistakable trend toward the elimination of almost all references to the senses, passion, and even fantasy. Here is a list of changes with the second version the final (substantive) one:

> line 45:   And the children are pulling,
>   On every side,
>   In a thousand vallies far and wide
>   Fresh flowers; . . .   (1807)
>   "pulling" changed to "culling" in 1836

> line 75:   At length the Man beholds it die away, . . .   (MS)

"beholds" changed to "perceives" in 1807

line 114:   Mighty Prophet! Seer blest!
                            On whom those truths do rest,
            Which we are toiling all our lives to find;
            Thou, over whom thy Immortality
            Broods like the Day, a Master o'er a Slave,
            A Presence which is not to be put by;
                            To whom the grave
            Is but a lonely bed without the sense or sight
                            Of day or the warm light,
            A place of thought where we in waiting lie; . . . (1807)
            "In darkness lost, the darkness of the grave"
            inserted after line 116 in 1820;
            lines 120–23 omitted in 1820;
            "place of thought" changed from "living place" in MS

line 129:   Full soon the soul shall have her earthy freight,
            The world upon thy noble nature seize,
            With all its varieties,   (MS)
            "the soul" changed to "thy soul" in 1807;
            "The world . . . varieties" omitted in 1807

line 155:   . . . a master light of all our seeing;
            Thrown off from us or mitigate our spell
            Of that strong frame of sense in which we dwell.
                            Uphold us, . . .   (MS)
            "Thrown off . . . we dwell" omitted in 1807

line 191:   Look not of any severing of our loves!   (MS)
            "Look not" changed to "Think not" in 1807;
            "Think not" changed to "Forbode not" in 1836

line 193:   I only have relinquished one delight
                            Divine indeed of sense
                            A blessed influence
            To acknowledge under you a higher sway   (MS)
            In 1807, changed to:
            I only have relinquished one delight
            To live beneath your more habitual sway

line 197:   The innocent brightness of a new-born Day
                            Is lovely yet;

Not unaccompanied with blithe desire,
Though many a serious pleasure it inspire   (MS)
"Not unaccompanied . . . inspire" omitted in 1807

line 200: The Clouds . . . awful colouring   (MS)
           "awful" becomes "sober" in 1807

line 204: Thanks to its tenderness, its joys, and fears   (1807)
           "joys" becomes "hopes" in 1849 MS

line 205: . . . the meanest flower that blows
           "meanest" becomes "humblest" in 1850 MS[1]

Perhaps the most revealing revision is the elimination of the phrase, "strong frame of sense in which we dwell." Like the definition of the child's power as a "might / Of untam'd pleasures," this line states emphatically that the body defines us and organizes our relationship to the world. This creates a problem for a poem which seeks consolation and preservation through disinterested contemplation. Not surprisingly, therefore, response to the world changes from sensuous apprehension (looking, beholding) to purer forms of mentation (perceiving, thinking). "The world," perceived "with all its varieties" through the senses disappears; it is no longer a "living place" but a "place of thought." Oxymoronic phrases which mark the poet's initial confusion over heavenly versus bodily definition are eliminated: "Divine indeed of sense," "blithe desire," "serious pleasure." Lines 120–23, exhibiting gothic fantasies of death as the loss of sensation, also eventually disappear.

In spite of the unease which the earlier versions of the poem produced in my students, the later, consistent version left most of them with some disappointment. A few saw the changes as strengthening the poem, confirming the poet's commitment to spirituality, even the (barely stated) afterlife. But most greeted the reduction in intellectual tension with the knowledge that something important both about life and about the experience of a poem had been abandoned. Less willing than before to yield to the comforts of literary consolation, they began to look for

1. The last two revisions are only in manuscripts, not in published editions.

more evidence that they were witnessing and participating in a genuine phenomenon of literary history. We turned next to the revision of the title and epigraph. The early title, "Ode," focused (as I have already suggested) the reader's attention on the genre of the poem and the tradition of odes. But also, put negatively, it refused to allow the reader to enter the poem concerned with a *subject*. Instead, to experience this poem consciously would be to concern oneself with *meaning*. That is, the pursuit of meaning without the presence of a subject activates the quest for understanding with no mediating, conciliating, and conclusive idealization of understanding through the presence of the poem's subject. Conceivably, Wordsworth, in 1815, wanted to short-circuit this process and guide the reader to interpret or overinterpret specific parts of the poem to the exclusion or subordination of others. In light of the revisions just observed, the revision of the title suggests that he wished to foreclose not multiple interpretations but precisely the recognition of the warring elements in his own vision.[2] Thus the revision of the title exactly reinforces the verbal revisions in the poem itself. The content of the new title, "Ode: Intimations of Immortality from Recollections of Early Childhood," further guides us to emphasize some aspects of the poem while deemphasizing others.

The title asks the reader to think about specific stages of life and about specific acts of mind. The stages are early childhood and an immortality which, from the construction of the title along the time line (early childhood and later, when recollection is possible), suggest before mortal life and perhaps after it. The middle of life exists in the title only as a position from which one can recall the past; otherwise it has no substantiality. The acts of mind are recollection and intimation. This is curious when one lists empirically the extraordinary range of other mental activities in the poem: analysis, apocalyptic discovery, questioning,

2. By far the finest and most detailed study of the revision of title and epigraph is Peter J. Manning's "Wordsworth's Intimations Ode and its Epigraphs," *Journal of English and Germanic Philology* 82 (1983): 526–40. I am indebted to this article for some of the following observations.

apostrophe, praise, self-consolation, self-conscious reflection, myth making, imaginative reconstruction, not to speak of the poem's range of moods from despair to joy. Perhaps most of all the title leaves out fantasy, which though reduced in the later editions (interestingly, after 1815 when the title was expanded), is nonetheless part of the landscape of the poem. Recollection and intimation act upon past and future, not upon the present. They assume, in fact, that the past and future have more reality than the present and draw the person out of the present into a more compelling time. A person is relatively passive (some might wish to say "receptive") in recollection and intimation and relatively unselfconscious and unanalytic. Wordsworth's late revision of "Think not" to "Forbode not" makes, in this context, perfect sense.

Since the poem does not actually exclude all these acts of mind, one must conclude that the title serves to subordinate their importance beneath that of recollection and intimation. The former do not define the condition of the speaker but are accessory to the latter, themselves relatively insignificant. But it is precisely all these acts of mind that comprise the mental activity of the adolescent and adult in the middle of life, who is in the process of establishing a sense of selfhood and a relationship to all the experiences of life. Thus the adolescent/adult acts and thinks in the poem but is not acknowledged; he is (from the intention of the title) a kind of negative space. (Hazlitt, to anticipate our later discussion, seems to register this when he renames the poem "Ode on the Progress of Life.")

The revision of epigraphs records a similar refocusing of the reader's consciousness and priorities. Just as the title of the 1807 edition refers us first of all to form and not to content, so the 1807 epigraph, *paulo maiora canamus* ("let us sing a little higher") refers to form. The phrase from Virgil's *Fourth Eclogue* states the limitation of the pastoral for accommodating the material of his poem, the heralding of a new Golden Age and the poet's role in realizing it —a subject which predicts the genre of epic. The important line is:

> si canimus silvas, silvae sint consule dignae.

> [If we must sing of woodlands, let them be worthy of a consul.]

The pastoral genre, conceived first as apolitical, is now reconceived as political and prophetic. Surely something like the reverse of this movement is implied in Wordsworth's reconception of the "Ode": far from becoming more political, it is changing from a more political to a "universal" theme, assuming beneath any drama of the moment a concern with "human nature." Wordsworth also, untypically, changes the "Ode" to include an elaborate analysis of human nature.

How do we understand thematically the association to Virgil's *Eclogue?* This poem describes the advent of a new Golden Age in terms of the birth of a savior child whose future is bound up with this new age. The poet enters the poem as subject only at the end and only to imagine his own glory and superiority over all other great poets if granted the opportunity to record the greatness of the golden age brought about by the maturing of the young child. So, like the traditional ode, Virgil's *Eclogue* focuses on the conservation of the image of the hero as other, and he himself as poet stands at a distance from his act. In this sense it differs from Wordsworth's "Ode," in which the poet's future and present bear the entire weight of the poem. Both poems, then, organize themselves around the fate of a young child, but the obvious difference is that the tradition of the fall from innocence from childhood to adulthood does not appear in the *Eclogue.* Growing up, for Virgil's child, is the evolution of a public (and a maturely sexual) figure of power and vision. The return of innocence operates on the public, social level. This is very like the predicted fate of Milton's Christ child. On the personal level the child does not engage in a struggle with the parent. No issue about guilt arises, nor is the child a figure of paradox (as in Wordsworth's "Mighty Prophet! Seer blest," "best philosopher," etc.), a child named as a nonchild. The Golden Age in Virgil is public and social; in Wordsworth the Golden Age belongs to the poet's private achievement, as he reasserts his connection to childhood. Virgil envisions in the Golden Age an economy of self-sufficiency in the produce from the natural world. Wordsworth's economy of self-sufficiency means that the self, as a metaphysical and psychological construct, does not require for its continuity a society at all, other than that of nature and children.

Wordsworth revised the epigraph to turn the emphasis from form to content:

> The Child is Father of the Man;
> And I could wish my days to be
> Bound each to each by natural piety.

The reader does not see the theme of the poem straining against the form. The form contains the content easily.

Wordsworth also dissolves the thematic contrasts between his poem and Virgil's. The 1815 epigraph seals the implications of the new title, focusing on generation as the limits of the poet's concern and extending that concern not (as in Virgil) into politics but into "natural piety." I say that the first line, "The Child is Father of the Man," is about generation, but actually it dismantles the historicity assumed in generation: the strivings, competitions, misunderstandings, separations, and also energies which the parent-child relationship rescues. It does something fairly common in eighteenth-century and early nineteenth-century poetry; it turns that relationship into a metaphor of itself. If you say that the child is father of the man, you say the child is *like* the father in some way, and you thereby undermine the actual historicity of the relationship. That historical relationship is metaphorized in the "Ode" proper (particularly section 8). The line predicts an ahistorical poem. The connector "and" creates the parallelism of the first phrase with the rest of the sentence. The ahistoricity of the first clause parallels the postulation of a wish. Wishes are part of history, particularly this wish, which is for a sameness of existence associated in Wordsworth to the mother or her substitute, Mother Nature. This wish itself is for an ahistorical permanence. Just as the phrase, "The Child is Father of the Man," moves toward an ahistoricity and is paradoxical in its construction, so there is a paradox of ahistoricity in the final two lines: "And I could wish my days to be / Bound each to each by natural piety." For on the one hand the line suggests the unchanging connection to nature. At the same time the word "piety" indicates the *will* to become pious. But the wish postulated is not a wish for the will but a wish of passivity and a displacement from the self to the time of life. It is as if he wants his time ("my days") to be bound by another force. By contrast the Virgilian epigraph asserts the force of the human will, the will to stretch the form of the poem to meet the new content, a new poetic and political reality. Having studied the ode tradition, the students could feel the massive significance of Virgil's phrase, Wordsworth's appropriation of it, and then his substitution.

13 "The Mad Monk" and Erotic Fantasy

Successive revisions of a poem, from early notebook entries to the final, "authoritative" lifetime edition, comprise only one type of revision. A reading of Wordsworth's "Ode" in the context of his earlier verse reveals that the poet provided himself with models and associations from his own repertoire that haunted him but allowed him to rethink these poems and their ideas within the tendency taken by his thinking. The apolitical rhetoric of the "Ode"—apolitical in terms of actual political reference and in terms of the explorations of passion and fantasy as part of radical literary representation—is a revision, a swerving away from the rhetoric and themes of his earlier poetry. For the students, the study of this kind of revision (added to the study of textual revision and the study of the ode tradition) further called into question the autonomy and authority of the "Ode."

The earlier poem most dramatically relevant to the "Ode" is "The Voice from the Side of Etna; or, The Mad Monk." First published in 1800 in the *Morning Post,* "The Mad Monk" had for a long time been thought to be a composition by Coleridge, but the recent scholarly efforts of Stephen M. Parrish and David V. Erdman point toward Wordsworth as author.[1] Regardless, the

1. David V. Erdman and Stephen M. Parrish, "Who Wrote 'The Mad Monk'?" *Bulletin of the New York Public Library* 64 (1960): 209–37.

poem clearly was readily available to Wordsworth. (In fact, the
uncertainty of authorship helped pedagogically to weaken for the
students the prejudice about authorship: i.e., if it is by Wordsworth it must be good, or important for the "Ode," and, conversely, if it is by Coleridge it must be less so.) Clearly it is important; the second section of the poem unmistakably is the model
upon which Wordsworth based the opening section of the "Ode":

> The Voice from the Side of Etna;
> or, The Mad Monk
> An Ode, in Mrs Radcliff's manner.
>
> I heard a voice from Etna's side,
>   Where o'er a Cavern's mouth,
>   That fronted to the South,
> A chestnut spread its umbrage wide.
> A Hermit, or a Monk, the man might be,
> But him I could not see:
> And thus the music flowed along,
> In melody most like an old Sicilian song.
>
> There was a time when earth, and sea, and skies,
>   The bright green vale and forest's dark recess,
> When all things lay before my eyes
>   In steady loveliness.
> But now I feel on earth's uneasy scene
>   Such motions as will never cease!
>   I only ask for peace —
> Then wherefore must I know, that such a time has been?
>
>   A silence then ensued.
>   Till from the cavern came
>   A voice. It was the same:
> And thus that mournful voice its dreary plaint renewed.
> Last night, as o'er the sloping turf I trod,
>   The smooth green turf to me a vision gave:
>   Beneath my eyes I saw the sod,
>   The roof of ROSA'S grave.
>
>   My heart has need with dreams like these to strive,
> For when I waked, beneath my eyes I found

That plot of mossy ground,
On which so soft we sate when ROSA was alive.
Why must the rock, and margin of the flood,
Why must the hills so many flowerets bear,
Whose colours to a wounded woman's blood
Such sad resemblance wear?

I struck the wound — this hand of mine!
For, oh! thou Maid divine,
I loved to agony!
The youth, whom thou call'dst thine,
Did never love like me.

It is the stormy clouds above,
That flash so red a gleam
On yonder downward trickling stream;
'Tis not the blood of her I love.
The sun torments me from his western bed!
O let him cease for ever to diffuse
Those crimson spectre hues!
O let me lie in peace, and be for ever dead!

Here ceased the voice! In deep dismay,
Down through the forest I pursued my way.
The twilight fays came forth in dewy shoon,
Ere I within the cabin had withdrawn,
The goat-herd's tent upon the open lawn.
That night there was no moon!![2]

Both the second section here and the first in the "Ode" call up the tradition of an innocence which, over the course of time, has been supplanted. Innocence in both poems appears as the look of the natural world. In the earlier poem this look is a "steady loveliness," but in the "Ode" it is the appearance of a "celestial light" in which nature is apparelled. The later poem introduces an association to a divine visionary presence; the earlier one defines innocence as continuity and continuity itself as beauty. The

2. William Wordsworth, *The Poems,* ed. John O. Hayden (New Haven: Yale University Press, 1981), 421–22.

loss of this condition in "The Mad Monk" means discontinuity and motion, which immediately generates the telling inner state of unease. The loss in the "Ode" simply creates an absence of what once was, or—and this is important—what *seemed* to be. The change in the earlier poem suggests that something in the real world happened to the speaker which affected him to the point that he can't refrain from wanting to recover what he has lost, now called "peace" or, the ceasing of the uneasy motion. We do not know what effect the change has had on the speaker of the "Ode"; we do not even know if the change happened in reality or in his own mind. That the speaker of the early poem is a hermit or monk, and is here and at the end called a voice, instructs us to see him as at least isolated and probably alienated. The speaker in the "Ode," while thoroughly solitary, is never alienated; the loss of "innocence" does not produce alienation, but in "The Mad Monk" it does.

The loss in "The Mad Monk" belongs to history and biography. In the "Ode" it belongs to a theological paradigm: the loss of divine or divinely sanctioned innocence. It is a version of the story of the Fall and as such refers finally not to particularity of individual and circumstance but to humanity. Moreover, the loss of the gleam has not been occasioned by an event but by biological and social development in the human condition. This noteworthy revision must be further specified: what precisely happened to the Mad Monk? Or, what story of loss did Wordsworth abandon when he wrote the "Ode"? It was a story of the jealous, murderous rage of a lover, a story of passion and sexual/aggressive fantasy leading to the awful act, the fulfilling of the fantasy in real life. The character fixes himself permanently in the psychological condition of his assault on his beloved: fantasy and reality merge, nature—far from a "homely Muse" or a playmate—takes on the uneasy motions of his guilt-ridden mind. This is the "Ode, in Mrs Radcliff's manner," a gothic drama in which nature is laced with the haunted, isolating passions of love.

Most obviously or implicitly radical literature of the late eighteenth century explores sexual passion and fantasy. In an age of revolution the destabilizing temperament of a social critic or activist often represented itself as some sort of triangular entanglement demanding, for satisfaction, the overthrow or annihilation of one of the conflicting members. What we now call the Oedipal triangle, in the eighteenth century usually exists with revolutionary resonances to sexual or class politics. "The Mad Monk" recapitulates in lyric form a common fantasy of the radical person. No distance or disinterestedness is possible, even if it is the not-so-hidden wish of the participant. Thus the narrator at the end of the poem can discover no consolation from or in spite of the story he has heard, a story which burdens him with a dismaying isolation caught from the alienated voice of the lover. The gloom at the end of the poem represents, in this period, a stage of radical consciousness which includes a (perhaps frightened) recognition of the social, destabilizing power of sexual fantasy, and as such it is a recognition of female consciousness which gothic romance activates. Wordsworth's recasting of this theme of loss without reference to sexual politics is comparable to his recasting of *The Prelude* with the omission of the Vaudracour and Julia episode: the story of a man's *Bildung* is much more consoling and confirming when it does not to account for the destabilizing and complicating presence of sexual fantasy and drama. The story of Vaudracour and Julia, a veiled retelling of Wordsworth's own shattering affair with Annette Vallon in 1792, is a sexual tragedy based upon a clash of aristocratic and bourgeois affiliations, a clash which—in the tradition of the eighteenth-century romantic novel—a class-constituted community cannot tolerate.

Wordsworth also changes the central focus from an adolescent or young adult, whose sexual fantasies and consciousness issue in action, to the young child who in the post-Rousseauian mind lives amidst a happiness or bliss devoid of fantasy and desire. Loss, then, is loss of that posited state of pure or chaste happiness. At this point I showed the students some of Blake's engravings from the *Songs of Innocence and Experience* in which songs of or about innocent childhood are illustrated with figures of sexual desire. Here, and on the frontispiece to *The Book of Thel* and on plate 3 of *Visions of the Daughters of Albion,* innocence is surprised to discover a vibrant eros in a wrongly assumed chasteness of its domain. One can interpret these engravings both with the Freudian hindsight that children in fact do have sexual desire, and, more appropriate historically, that the engravings explore adult wishes to transfer happiness to an idyllic space without desire, a wish that conforms to eighteenth-century constructions of patriarchal happiness. Also, the representation of sexual desire naturally assumes the fantasies of desire, or just *fantasy* itself. Very simply, "The Mad Monk" is the fantasy which "The Immortality Ode" abandons and (as Hazlitt will show) replaces with the doctrine of preexistence.

Like the revisions he made in the manuscripts and editions, the changes from "The Mad Monk" to the "Ode" move in the direction of a consistently evolving male-dominant identity, one that is confirmed through the benign echoes of an idyllic nature. The person sheds passion and fantasy as stages of biological and social development superficial to the perdurable core of "human" nature.[3]

3. See my essay, "The Immortality Ode: Lionel Trilling and Helen Vendler," *The Wordsworth Circle* 12 (1981): 64–70, for a demonstration of the "Ode"'s echoes from Wordsworth's political sonnets of 1801–2. Language set in a poetry of historical moment is recast in the ahistorical context of the "Ode."

From William Blake's *Songs of Innocence and of Experience,* plate 25.

129

From *The Illuminated Blake,* annotated by David V. Erdman, Garden City, New York: Anchor, Doubleday, 1974, plate 34.

130

The Argument

I loved Theotormon
And I was not ashamed
I trembled in my virgin fears
And I hid in Leutha's vale

I plucked Leutha's flower,
And I rose up from the vale
But the terrible thunders tore
My virgin mantle in twain

From *The Illuminated Blake,* plate 128.

131

Part Five
Biography and History

14 The "Ode" and Wordsworth's Biography

By this time my students saw quite clearly that the elimination of references to the senses, passion, fantasy, and contemporary political concern all seemed an undeniable direction taken by the poem. Many were made uneasy or defensive because the study of revisions and "The Mad Monk" threw into question the integrity or "purity" of the poem as an act of consolation or spiritualization. It was hard to believe in a spontaneity inherent in Wordsworth's spiritualizing art; instead it seemed derivative. Passion and fantasy began to assume the unsettling power usually denied them; how can poetry, that chaste and sacred realm, mount a crisis around something this explosive? It was now that I thought of Trilling's essay "On the Teaching of Modern Literature," with its complaint about the ease with which his students could "look into the abyss" of Joyce or Kafka or Conrad and come up smiling. No such complacency followed the uncovering of these "impure" impulses in a text with which they thought they could identify through a consoling intention.

One needs to avoid the too-easy assumption that these young people responded to this demystification of consolation either with total defensiveness or total acceptance. Their response was ambivalent, reflecting, I believe, what are usually taken to be the two major aspects of adolescent identity formation (see, for example, Erikson, Blos): the "self-aspect" in which consolidation

135

of identity refers to the regulation of id and super-ego, and the "ego-aspect" (Erikson) which refers to consolidation with respect to the larger, social world. The "Ode" in its final version speaks primarily to the former aspect, the integrity of self without reference to the world and to issues beyond the self, but the "Ode" in the context of its revisions raises issues relevant to the latter aspect. Put more simply, consciousness of the revisions stimulates both a need to protect oneself from the implications of them and simultaneously an urge to engage those implications. Further, in the language of Horkheimer and Adorno, the students experience the opposing drives of self-integration and self-abandonment.

Unquestionably the drive of self-integration expressed itself in the students' particular extravagant rhetoric and perilous language, not unpredictable at any time but particularly notable in this fundamentalist decade. Most notable was the emergence of a language of ritualistic purification around the problem of revision. Wordsworth, by revising out the associations to sense and passion, "purified" the poem. Conversely, those same associations, said another student, "polluted" it. These were not casually chosen verbs but were accurate interpretations, from Wordsworth's point of view (in all likelihood) as well as their own, of what these revisions meant. They further reinforced the Christian atmosphere which emanates from the poem and from the wishes and assumptions of many students in the presence of poetry. The poet's choice lies in purification of the impure, driving out the extraneous, the benighted impediments to a "spiritual" exercise, and in first valuing the early associations as impurities. The same teleology of the poem applies to the poet's character. One day a student muttered about Wordsworth's biography: "soon we will learn that Wordsworth, as a young man, was homosexual," a comment richly denigrating; his youth, perverted — or because of his youth's great confusion of passions, perverted — demanded the purification it eventually received.

But many students held up to this self-protective and defensive posture a compelling curiosity about the origins of his associations to fantasy and passion and of his later refusal to commit further to these associations. They began to search for the social and historical meaning of his choices. Biography and history, usually imported into classroom analyses of literature out of a sense of duty or decorum, were now valued through the students' own instincts about the historical basis of art; on this subject I needed to deliver no solemn speech.

In presenting biography and history to students who were thus sensitized to the suppressions and omissions in the "Ode," and who saw revisions occurring in time (i.e., the successive dates of publication), I was tempted to organize Wordsworth's life as a kind of psychohistorical analysis that would show a life begun in a passion and an abandon that traumatic experience thwarted or annulled. But I started with some testimony that seemed to support the notion of the purity and primary position of the poem's final spirituality—first, the famous remarks from the Fenwick Note about the "abyss of idealism":

> . . . it was not so much from [feelings] of animal vivacity that *my* difficulty came as from a sense of the indomitableness of the spirit within me. I used to brood over the stories of Enoch and Elijah, and almost to persuade myself that, whatever might become of others, I should be translated, in something of the same way, to heaven. With a feeling congenial to this, I was often unable to think of external things as having external existence, and I communed with all that I saw as something not apart from, but inherent in, my own immaterial nature. Many times while going to school have I grasped at a wall or tree to recall myself from this abyss of idealism to the reality.[1]

And from Christopher Wordsworth's *Memoirs:* "I record my own feelings at that time—my absolute spirituality, my 'all-soulness,' if I may so speak." And Christopher Wordsworth brings forth further testimony from R. P. Graves:

> I remember Mr Wordsworth saying that, at a particular stage of his mental progress, he used to be frequently so rapt into an

1. Wordsworth, *The Poems,* ed. John O. Hayden (New Haven: Yale University Press, 1981), 979.

unreal transcendental world of ideas that the external world seemed no longer to exist in relation to him, and he had to reconvince himself of its existence by *clasping a tree,* or something that happened to be near him.[2]

Wordsworth, in later years, recalled or imagined his early years in the way of the poem's final version. Are we to doubt him, to question his memory or his later intentions? Surely "absolute spirituality" contradicts some of the definition of self in early versions of the "Ode." Yet he spoke with such conviction — and apparently to more than one person — about his own childhood experience that to contradict him seems arrogant: historical reconstruction of causes has, of course, its limits. At the same time Wordsworth's own memories are themselves a refashioning, and in this case the memory conforms to what the "late" Wordsworth *would* say. With this observation I began my own reconstruction of his life, which, for present purposes, I will not recapitulate in full but only highlight.

Childhood must have been a confusing mixture of plenty and scarcity, happiness and terror. Correspondingly, he found in nature an abundance and a warmth which must have registered with the comparable experience with his parents. Yet nature, described in *The Prelude,* is at times harsh, dangerous; life in it is exhilarating but precarious:

> Oh, when I have hung
> Above the raven's nest, by knots of grass
> Or half-inch fissures in the slipp'ry rock
> But ill sustained, and almost, as it seemed,
> Suspended by the blast which blew amain,
> Shouldering the naked crag, oh, at that time,
> While on the perilous ridge I hung alone,
> With what strange utterance did the loud dry wind
> Blow through my ears; the sky seemed not a sky
> Of earth, and with what motion moved the clouds![3]
>
> (1799; First Part, 57–66)

2. Ibid.
3. This and subsequent passages from Wordsworth's *The Prelude* from *The*

The child, unlike the conventional pastoral children in the "Ode," lives in the medium of nature, fully in contact with it, sexual and passionate: "I wheeled about / Proud and exulting, like an untired horse / That cares not for its home"; "we had given our bodies to the wind"; "as I rose upon the stroke my boat / Went heaving through the water like a swan. . . ."; "hurrying on, / Still hurrying, hurrying onward, how my heart / Panted . . . Sometimes strong desire / Resistless overpowered me, . . ." Nature is not indifferent to this energy; it responds in mysterious and terrifying ways:

> While on the perilous ridge I hung alone,
> With what strange utterance did the loud dry wind
> Blow through my ears; the sky seemed not a sky
> Of earth, and with what motion moved the clouds!
>
> (1799; First Part, 63–66)

> . . . from behind that rocky steep, till then
> The bound of the horizon, a huge cliff,
> As if with voluntary power instinct,·
> Upreared its head. I struck, and struck again,
> And, growing still in stature, the huge cliff
> Rose up between me and the stars, and still,
> With measured motion, like a living thing
> Stroke after me.
>
> (1799; First Part, 107–14)

> With the din,
> Meanwhile, the precipices rang aloud;
> The leafless trees and every icy crag
> Tinkled like iron; while the distant hills
> Into the tumult sent an alien sound
> Of melancholy, not unnoticed; while the stars,
> Eastward, were sparkling clear, and in the west
> The orange sky of evening died away.
>
> (1799; 162–69)

Prelude, 1799, 1805, 1850, ed. Jonathan Wordsworth et al. (New York: W. W. Norton, 1979).

And all the shadowy banks on either side
Came sweeping through the darkness, spinning still
The rapid line of motion, then at once
Have I, reclining back upon my heels
Stopped short — yet still the solitary cliffs
Wheeled by me, even as if the earth had rolled
With visible motion her diurnal round.

(1799; 176–82)

Yet the poet of 1799, now interpreting these events, sees such erotic adventures, full of desire and contact and the outsized mysteries and distortions of nature, as leading beyond that physical and mental extravagance to a place of peace and harmony or unity, a principle, really, of divine and benign order. This is the stated fullness, and it contrasts with the final desolation or "dreariness" of many of his actual childhood involvements. The story of his childhood is marked by an absence of the two figures one expects to hear about — his mother and father. I am not only thinking of their early deaths when the poet was eight and thirteen years old respectively, but that they must have not been *there* for him in important ways even earlier in life. This seems to have led to the peculiar mixture of idealization and terror of parental figures displaced onto nature. So many of the early experiences described end in a melancholy solitude which, without the healing power of time and some capacity to heal his own wounds, probably would have given him memories of harsh betrayals and blank absences.

The Prelude, on the other hand, gives (in book 2, 1805 and 1850 editions) the kernel of a pleasurable and full life of adolescent exuberance, sometimes in solitude but mostly with his proto-society of friends and acquaintances. This level of engagement resumes (by his account) in his 1790 trip to France with his friend Robert Jones to witness sympathetically the onset of the French Revolution in its initial optimism. When he returns to France in 1792, however, the precariousness of his social joy emerges. The romantic tragedy with his lover Annette Vallon, the onset of the Terror, and his own activism in the cause of Revolution

lead not to fulfillment but to the profound sense of betrayal and
emptiness as in the following passage describing his response to
the September (1792) massacres:

> 'The horse is taught his manage, and the wind
> Of heaven wheels round and treads in his own steps;
> Year follows year, the tide returns again,
> Day follows day, all things have second birth;
> The earthquake is not satisfied at once'—
> And in such way I wrought upon myself,
> Until I seemed to hear a voice that cried
> To the whole city, 'Sleep no more!' To this
> Add comments of a calmer mind—from which
> I could not gather full security—
> But at the best it seemed a place of fear,
> Unfit for the repose of night,
> Defenceless as a wood where tigers roam.
>
> (1805; book 10, lines 70–82)

"Defenceless" before the demise of several ideals, he returns to
England only to watch the English collaboration with the Conti-
nent against revolutionary France. If France became the collapsed
idealization of paternal strength and imagination, then England
became the collapsed substitute for maternal trust (in nature):

> As a light
> And pliant harebell, swinging in the breeze
> On some grey rock—its birth-place—so had I
> Wantoned, fast rooted on the ancient tower
> Of my beloved country, wishing not
> A happier fortune than to wither there:
> Now was I from that pleasant station torn
> And tossed about in whirlwind.
>
> (1850; book 10, lines 276–83)

This version of his experiences in France and England from
1792 to 1794 was, of course, written much later, in fact during
the time of the completion of the "Ode." It was important for

me to emphasize to the students the intensely passionate and radical level of Wordsworth's engagement with love and international politics. His affair with Annette Vallon may have been the single daring act of love in his life and has at its center the bliss and entangled consequence of *Clarissa, Julie,* and *Werther.* Here is Annette's letter to Dorothy Wordsworth after William has left:

> I cannot be happy without him, I desire him every day, but I shall have plenty of reasons for submitting to the lot which I must undergo. I often call to my aid that reason which too often is weak and powerless beside my feelings for him: no, my dear friend, he will never picture justly the need I have of him to make me happy; mastered by a feeling which causes all my unhappiness. I cherish always his dominion over me, and the influence of his dear love on my heart which is always concerned with him. His image follows me everywhere; often when I am alone in my room with his letters I think he has entered. . . . Ah my dear sister this is my continual state; emerging from my mistake as from a dream I see him not, the father of my child; he is very far from me. This scene is often repeated and throws me into extreme melancholy.[4]

Similarly, Wordsworth wrote "A Letter to the Bishop of Llandaff" (1793) as an open attack on monarchy, hereditary nobility, the plight of the poor, and the effect of war on the poor, which placed him in the radical camp of, among others, Tom Paine. If, in addition, he sympathized with plotters to assassinate Louis XVI and with those English radicals planning in France to launch a military invasion of England, then Wordsworth's life was at this time highly destabilized and committed. But the disappointments in all these activities led to an enormous retrenchment and reorganization of his goals and (like other young Romantics) his interpretations of experience; in this new way he seems to have found the beginnings of equanimity. Politically, Burke's writings began to influence him decisively; the new acquaintance with the religious Coleridge — for the time being comfortable with a

4. Mary Moorman, *William Wordsworth: A Biography* (London: Oxford University Press, 1957), 1:181.

new version of the eighteenth-century aesthetics of rural retirement — helped slowly to settle Wordsworth toward his own more
conservative poetics (or as Peter J. Manning has recently suggested, to *return* him to the conservative world view in which he
had been raised); but just prior to both of these influences was
the return to his sister Dorothy and their decision to make a life
together. The passage in *The Prelude,* again written during the
period of the "Ode," marks the clear shift of his passions and
intellect:

> And then it was
> That the belovèd woman in whose sight
> Those days were passed — now speaking in a voice
> Of sudden admonition like a brook
> That does but cross a lonely road; and now
> Seen, heard and felt, and caught at every turn,
> Companion never lost through many a league —
> Maintained for me a saving intercourse
> With my true self (for, though impaired, and changed
> Much, as it seemed, I was no further changed
> Than as a clouded, not a waning moon);
> She, in the midst of all, preserved me still
> A poet, made me seek beneath that name
> My office upon earth, and nowhere else.
> And lastly, Nature's self, by human love
> Assisted, through the weary labyrinth
> Conducted me again to open day,
> Revived the feelings of my earlier life,
> Gave me that strength and knowledge full of peace,
> Enlarged, and never more to be disturbed, . . .
>   (1805; book 10, lines 907–26)

Here Wordsworth states that his identity as a poet comes from
his own family, from the tie to the natural world, and stands op-
posed to the fluctuations of passion-love and radical political activism. *The Prelude* accurately subordinates such involvements and
commitments to the ephemeral and the anomalous, like a cloud
momentarily and erratically covering the steady heartless light
of the moon. Not irrelevant to the young people listening to this

moving story is its lesson for the successful achievement of identity: a recovery of an "essential" self to be found through domestic love and the innocent pleasures in (what has become) an idyllic nature. Equally, however, they marked the abandonments that his new peace exacted.

Changes in political sympathy and personal pressures dovetail in the decade 1792–1802. Wordsworth left an activist life for a domestic and religious life in retirement; his politics moved from radical (no matter how temporary that radicalism was) to increasingly conservative. Biographically, the years of the writing of the "Ode," 1802–4, contained a mix of happiness and anxiety, contentment and physical and mental discomfort. Settling into the steady life of Dove Cottage hardly steadied the inner lives of the poet and his family. William was beset with headaches and pains and anxious about his upcoming marriage (October 1802). But for four or five years the "counter-revolutionary" period in England, directed philosophically by the "genius of Burke," began to exert over Wordsworth a calming and restorative influence; and the poet experienced what Burke called "the happy effect of following Nature, which is wisdom without reflection, and above it."[5] A revolutionary age and temperament is characterized by disruptions and passions; Burke ascribed to a national temperament of calm, of asserting and valuing the links of tradition and custom. Following him, Wordsworth celebrated living beneath the "habitual sway" of nature. The value of time, as marking the points of change or reform or revolution, yields to the value of timelessness and to the celebration of life for its continuities instead of its instances of momentous mental exertion toward change. He created more and more a poetry of the "affections," of calm inner states creative of and created by the idyllic beauty of the Vale of Grasmere and its surroundings. Dorothy Wordsworth registered in her Journals the intenser responses to beauty and pleasure: "Grasmere looked so beautiful that my heart was almost melted away" (21 June 1800).

5. Quoted in James K. Chandler, *Wordsworth's Second Nature* (Chicago: University of Chicago Press, 1984), 73.

"We came down and rested upon a moss covered Rock, rising out of the bed of the River. There we lay ate our dinner and stayed there till about 4 o'clock or later. Wm and C. repeated and read verses. I drank a little Brandy and water and was in Heaven" (4 May 1802).[6] William, in contrast, wrote, on 21 May 1807 (in a letter to the wife of his patron George Beaumont about calming, idyllic, "permanent affections" in the section of *Poems, in Two Volumes* called "Moods of My Own Mind":

> There is scarcely a Poem here of above thirty Lines, and very trifling these poems will appear to many; but, omitting to speak of them individually, do they not, taken collectively, fix the attention upon a subject eminently poetical, viz., the interest which objects in nature derive from the predominance of certain affections more or less permanent, more or less capable of salutary renewal in the mind of the being contemplating these objects?[7]

The purpose of these poems is "to console the afflicted, to add sunshine to daylight by making the happy happier, to teach the young and the gracious of every age, to see, to think and feel, and therefore to become more actively and securely virtuous. . . ." The concern to encourage "permanent" affections, that the effect of his poetry "must be a work *of time*," that the value of the spontaneous encounter exists only when the social or psychological vividness of the moment dwindles before the deeper feelings of peace, all this reflects not only a need to dwell in such idyllic permanence but also a desire to *create*, as Rousseau said, a "sentiment of being." The "calm so deep" felt while the poet stands on Westminster Bridge (1802) surfaces because what makes the city urban still sleeps and the air is still (rurally) smokeless. Indeed, the idyllic permanence of the calm feeling seems to need our proleptic knowledge of the urban assault of commerce and

6. *Journals of Dorothy Wordsworth*, ed. Mary Moorman (London: Oxford University Press, 1971), 29, 120.

7. *The Letters of William and Dorothy Wordsworth*, ed. Ernest de Selincourt; rev. Mary Moorman (Oxford: Clarendon, 1969), vol. 2, *The Middle Years, 1806–1811*, 146, 50.

human variety. In "To the Cuckoo" the present, evoked by the sound of the early-springtime bird, immediately turns to autobiographical comparison (past and present) in order to assert that when an event of the moment reaches to the "sentiment of being," time is no time:

O blithe New-comer! I have heard,
I hear thee and rejoice.
O Cuckoo! shall I call thee Bird,
Or but a wandering Voice?

While I am lying on the grass
Thy twofold shout I hear,
From hill to hill it seems to pass
At once far off, and near.

Though babbling only to the Vale,
Of sunshine and of flowers,
Thou bringest unto me a tale
Of visionary hours.

Thrice welcome, darling of the Spring!
Even yet thou art to me
No bird, but an invisible thing,
A voice, a mystery;

The same whom in my schoolboy days
I listened to; that Cry
Which made me look a thousand ways
In bush, and tree, and sky.

To seek thee did I often rove
Through woods and on the green;
And thou wert still a hope, a love;
Still longed for, never seen.

And I can listen to thee yet;
Can lie upon the plain
And listen, till I do beget
That golden time again.

O blessèd Bird! the earth we pace
Again appears to be

An unsubstantial, faery place;
That is fit home for Thee!

The poem plays games with time. It passes over the "school-boy days" of ascending adolescent passion to replace them with the serene passivity of the present adult who has a very active, synthesizing, and idyllicizing imagination. Even the sexual reference in "*beget* that golden time" works to efface a sexual imagination with its appearance. And creation, begetting, is really a re-creation (beget *again*). Autobiographical comparison turns the sexual moment of creation into a spiritualized harmony of past and present.

After having reviewed the history of Western Europe and England during and following the French Revolution, and after having become acquainted with Wordsworth's biography from birth until the publication of the 1815 edition of poems, the students returned to the "Ode." Does this poem "make sense," I asked, in light of history and biography? One student thought that it made less sense than Coleridge's "Departing Year" or, even more, "France: An Ode," which demonstrated the individual's reaction to an historical development, and to which the "Ode" makes no reference. A second student, however, saw the "Ode" as responsive to history defined as a series of traumatic disruptions: the death of his parents, the betrayal of the Revolution, the loss of Annette and Caroline Vallon. The "Ode," she observed, is precisely not these things. The absence of history and erotic love, given their cataclysmic results for Wordsworth, seems to allow for a vision of continuities and coherence. He gives himself childhood and a maturity that strengthen and reaffirm each other. In an early poem, "The Convict," Wordsworth expressed the wish to "plant" this person beaten down by history, "in a different soil," to give him a new lifestory that has the organic coherence of the vegetable world. In the "Ode" he completes this task for himself.

Wordsworth seems to have advanced the cause of internal peace successfully in his poetry and life during the first decade of the nineteenth century. His poetry, and his increasingly religious orientation, helped to create the ideology of the Romantic poet as an embodiment as well as a celebrant of pure human nature. The reviewers of *Poems, in Two Volumes* did not like it, particularly the section "Moods of My Own Mind," finding the subjects of the poems "trivial" and the exploration of moods themselves as "unmanly": thus "The Happy Warrior" received more praise than a poem like "To the Cuckoo." But the poet himself began to define his sympathetic readership to accommodate such criticism, or, as he thought it, misunderstanding: ". . . to be incapable of a feeling of Poetry in my sense of the word is to be without love of human nature and reverence for God."[8] Obviously such people abound; the Romantic poetic ideology demands such a restriction of membership to these who are not "dull of soul." Armed with this ideology and an increasingly secure domestic life (with children), Wordsworth moves closer to the revisions of the "Ode" in 1815 and 1820. But surely the deaths of two young children, Catherine and Thomas, increase the urgency of his poetry of consolation. Indeed, the loss of Catherine, inspiring the beautiful sonnet "Surprised by joy—impatient as the Wind" (1813), though it did not initiate it, may have confirmed the change in the association of the child composed of "untam'd passions" to one composed with "might Of heav'n born freedom":

> Through what power,
> Even for the least division of an hour,
> Have I been so beguiled as to be blind
> To my most grievous loss!—That thought's return
> Was the worst pang that sorrow ever bore,
> Save one, one only, when I stood forlorn,
> Knowing my heart's best treasure was no more;
> That neither present time, nor years unborn
> Could to my sight that heavenly face restore.

A footnote to the biography from 1810 to 1812 and presumably therefore of the entire period is required for the discussion of sexual passion, or its striking absence in his poetry. The recently discovered love letters of William and Mary Wordsworth,

8. Ibid., 146.

edited in a volume by Beth Darlington, make clear that Wordsworth in no way lacked for animal spirits and passionate love
for his wife:

> Oh my beloved — but I ought not to trust myself to this senseless
> & visible sheet of paper; speak for me to thyself, find the evi-
> dence of what is passing within me in *thy* heart, in thy mind, in
> thy steps as they touch the green grass, in thy limbs as they are
> stretched upon the soft earth; in thy own involuntary sighs &
> ejaculations, in the trembling of thy hands, in the tottering of
> thy lips themselves, & such kisses as I often give to the empty
> air, and in the aching of thy bosom, and let a voice speak for
> me in every thing within thee & without thee.[9]
>
> (3–4 June 1812)

The absence of any such language or sentiment in the poetry
(1800–15) and, if anything, its decline from earlier years reinforces an important fact both of biography and of poetry: this
absence comes not from defensiveness or inhibition or personal
reticence but a conviction about the public function and the ideology of poetry. This makes all the more useful and trustworthy
Hazlitt's essentially political criticism of Wordsworth's refusal to
speak of passion in the "Ode."

9. *The Love Letters of William and Mary Wordsworth,* ed. Beth Darlington (London: Chatto and Windus, 1982), 229–30.

Part Six
Criticism from
a Contemporary

15   Hazlitt, Poetry, and Mr. Wordsworth

"Poetry is the language of the imagination and the passions."
"Poetry thus is an imitation of nature, but the imagination and
the passions are a part of man's nature." "Poetry is the high-
wrought enthusiasm of fancy and feeling."[1] William Hazlitt stands
as the most brilliant antagonist to Wordsworthian poetics in the
early nineteenth century. It is hard to discover a reader of Wordsworth in the past 175 years who dramatizes more acutely the problems for post-Enlightenment poets and their readers than Hazlitt.
The response of my students to Hazlitt has always been powerful, unsettling, and catalyzing. No critic can live so completely
in Wordsworth's power and charm, but no reader understands
and says so well that it *is* a charm, that it turns away from social
immediacy and the life of fantasy and passion as the lifeblood
of interpersonal relationships and tries to convince the reader
that the pure ether of solitude is more real. Hazlitt is the one
major cultural critic of the period to demonstrate again and
again the political content of passion and fantasy through which
one discerns the fundamentally social ("intersubjective" in John
Kinnaird's language) nature of human beings. To the degree
that he writes about an object eroticized by the observing sub-

1. *The Hazlitt Sampler,* ed. Herschel M. Sikes (Gloucester, Mass.: Peter Smith,
1969), 109–20.

ject, Wordsworth fulfills Hazlitt's demand for poetry. To the degree that he focuses more on the experience of the subject to the exclusion of the otherness and reality of the object, Wordsworth is an egotist and not a modern poet of high order. As long as beauty is not at the expense of either subject or object, as long as beauty exists not at the expense of fantasy or of critical consciousness, it confers upon the reader the blessing of mind consciously seeking its freedom and dignity in a repressive world. Mind, for Hazlitt, ideally exists (like his own relentless prose) in a constant search for social and personal truth; if poetic beauty does not serve that end, it ceases to further the highest needs of humanity and instead fosters the complacency and condescension of which Hazlitt often accused Wordsworth. Hazlitt has an insight about the appropriateness of mental freedom as the final object of modern totalitarian inclinations:

> It is not only the progress of mechanical knowledge, but the necessary advances of civilization, that are unfavourable to the spirit of poetry. We not only stand in less awe of the preternatural world, but we can calculate more surely, and look with more indifference, upon the regular routine of this. The heroes of the fabulous ages rid the world of monsters and giants. At present we are less exposed to the vicissitudes of good or evil, to the incursions of wild beasts or "bandit fierce," or to the unmitigated fury of the elements. The time has been that "our fell of hair would at a dismal treatise rouse and stir as life were in it." But the police spoils all; and we now hardly so much as dream of a midnight murder. Macbeth is only tolerated in this country for the sake of the music; and in the United States of America, where the philosophical principles of government are carried still farther in theory and practice, we find that the Beggars' Opera is hooted from the stage. Society, by degrees, is constructed into a machine that carries us safely and insipidly from one end of life to the other, in a very comfortable prose style.[2]

2. William Hazlitt, *Complete Works*, ed. P. P. Howe (London: J. M. Dent, 1930–34), 5:9–10.

The best poetry of the modern (or any) age would show its awareness of the centrality of passion and of the need to represent individuals in their social roles. Nowhere does he differentiate himself more clearly from Wordsworth than in this particular. Wordsworth says of the poet that he must give pleasure "to a human Being possessed of that information which may be expected from him, not as a lawyer, a physician, a mariner, an astronomer or a natural philosopher, but as a Man" (1802 *Preface*). By contrast Hazlitt says:

> The child is a poet, in fact, when he first plays at hide-and-seek, or repeats the story of Jack the Giant-killer; the shepherd-boy is a poet, when he first crowns his mistress with a garland of flowers; the countryman, when he stops to look at the rainbow; the city-apprentice, when he gazes after the Lord-Mayor's show; the miser, when he hugs his gold; the courtier, who builds his hopes upon a smile; the savage, who paints his idol with blood; the slave, who worships a tyrant, or the tyrant, who fancies himself a god; — the vain, the ambitious, the proud, the choleric man, the hero and the coward, the beggar and the king, the rich and the poor, the young and the old, all live in a world of their own making; and the poet does no more than describe what all the others think and act.[3]

Individuals are real in their roles, which implies they are so in their class relations. It follows, says Hazlitt, that "the sense of power is as strong a principle in the mind as the love of pleasure." In this he modifies and extends Wordsworth's claim that poetry speaks to the "grand elementary principle of pleasure." This formulation, like Rousseau's "sentiment of being," posits something more elemental than power; but if that something exists, it must not — when it appears in poetry — exclude reference to the power relation, or it ends by denying our social nature.

Early reviewers and critics of Wordsworth tended to see his poetry, usually suspiciously, as programmatic and therefore as

3. Ibid., 2.

tending to constrain rather than to liberate mind. Hazlitt ambivalently has the same suspicion that Wordsworth continually and increasingly sought to create a readership that concurred with his views. Both Wordsworth and Coleridge, for example, insisted that only a select group could respond to the "Ode." Said Coleridge in the *Biographia Literaria:* ". . . the ode was intended for such readers only as had been accustomed to watch the flux and reflux of their inmost nature, to venture at times into the twilight realms of consciousness, and to feel a deep interest in modes of inmost being, to which they know that the attributes of time and space are inapplicable and alien, but which yet can not be conveyed save in symbols of time and space."[4] Perhaps most important in Hazlitt's irritation with this feature of Wordsworth's poetry is the conviction that such a circle of sympathetic individuals existed only to exclude the many and to foster a perennial class elite.

Hazlitt's brilliant portrait of "Mr. Wordsworth" in *The Spirit of The Age* (1825) focuses in almost every detail on Wordsworth as a *poet of exclusions;* he is described by what he leaves out:

> He has "no figures nor no fantasies, which busy *passion* draws in the brains of men:" neither the gorgeous machinery or mythologic lore, nor the splendid colours of poetic diction. His style is vernacular: he delivers household truths. He sees nothing loftier than human hopes; nothing deeper than the human heart.

> His popular, inartificial style gets rid (at a blow) of all the trappings of verse, of all the high places of poetry: "the cloud-capt towers, the solemn temples, the gorgeous palaces," are swept to the ground, and "like the baseless fabric of a vision, leave not a wreck behind." All the traditions of learning, all the superstitions of age, are obliterated and effaced. We begin *de novo,* on a *tabula rasa* of poetry. The purple pall, the nodding plume of tragedy are exploded as mere pantomime and trick, to return to the simplicity of truth and nature. Kings, queens, priests, nobles, the altar and the throne, the distinctions of rank, birth,

---

4. Samuel Taylor Coleridge, *Biographia Literaria,* ed. J. Shawcross (London: Oxford University Press, 1967), 2:120.

wealth, power, "the judge's robe, the marshall's truncheon, the ceremony that to great ones 'longs," are not to be found here. The author tramples on the pride of art with greater pride. The Ode and Epode, the Strophe and the Antistrophe, he laughs to scorn. The harp of Homer, the trump of Pindar and of Alcaeus are still. The decencies of costume, the decorations of vanity are stripped off without mercy as barbarous, idle, and Gothic. The jewels in the crisped hair, the diadem on the polished brow are thought meretricious, theatrical, vulgar; and nothing contents his fastidious taste beyond a simple garland of flowers. Neither does he avail himself of the advantages which nature or accident hold out to him.

No storm, no shipwreck startles us by its horrors: but the rainbow lifts its head in the cloud, and the breeze sighs through the withered fern. No sad vicissitude of fate, no overwhelming catastrophe in nature deforms his page: but the dew-drop glitters on the bending flower, the tear collects in the glistening eye.[5]

This includes passion: "Reserved, yet haughty, having no unruly or violent passions, (or those passions having been early suppressed). . . ." And it includes the suppression, or exclusion, of variety: "His Muse . . . is a levelling one. It proceeds on a principle of equality, and strives to reduce all things to the same standard." An economy of poetic energy is at work, but in proportion to the principle of exclusion emerges the principle of subjectivity, reflection and memory, and spirituality. Everything "becomes an object of imagination to him." At his best he merges with the objects of nature: ". . . he has stopped to have a nearer view of the daisy under his feet, or plucked a branch of whitethorn from the spray; but in describing it, his mind seems imbued with the majesty and solemnity of the objects around him — the tall rock lifts its head in the erectness of his spirit: the cataract roars in the sound of his verse. . . ."

Hazlitt, in his effort to understand both the excluding and subjectivizing tendencies in Wordsworth's poetry, turns to biography:

5. Hazlitt, *Complete Works* 11:86–95, passim.

Possibly a good deal of this may be regarded as the effect of disappointed views and an inverted ambition. Prevented by native pride and indolence from climbing the ascent of learning or greatness, taught by political opinions to say to the vain pomp and glory of the world, "I hate ye," seeing the path of classical and artificial poetry blocked up by the cumbrous ornaments of style and turgid *commonplaces,* so that nothing more could be achieved in that direction but by the most ridiculous bombast or the tamest servility; he has turned back partly from the bias of his mind, partly perhaps from a judicious policy—has struck into the sequestered vale of humble life, sought out the Muse among sheepcotes and hamlets and the peasant's mountain-haunts, has discarded all the tinsel pageantry of verse, and endeavoured (not in vain) to aggrandise the trivial and add the charm of novelty to the familiar.[6]

How perceptive to discover that the poetry of subjectivity is not a "pure" or elemental impulse in Wordsworth but rather a reaction to and a compensation for "disappointed views"! Surely this is deeply true; nor does the fact that Hazlitt was "disappointed" in many of his contemporaries make his response to Wordsworth less true. Hazlitt did not know the effects on Wordsworth of parent-loss and of disappointment in love; he is aware of his disappointment (or betrayal) in the French Revolution and radical politics, the disappointment in England itself.

6. Ibid.

16 Hazlitt, *Romeo and Juliet,* and the "Ode"

Hazlitt's main discussion of the "Ode" appears as an extended digression in, surprisingly, his lecture on Shakespeare's *Romeo and Juliet.* Yet the consistency of Hazlitt's thinking about poetry and his preoccupation with the difficulties, for him, in Wordsworth's poetry ought to make his outburst seem less gratuitous. Hazlitt, to begin with, admires Shakespeare for his, and *Romeo and Juliet* for its, passion:

> Romeo and Juliet are in love, but they are not love-sick. Every thing speaks the very soul of pleasure, the high and healthy pulse of the passions: the heart beats, the blood circulates and mantles throughout.[1]

Their young love, he observes, belongs to the future, and therefore to fantasy:

> He has founded the passion of the two lovers not on the pleasures they had experienced, but on all the pleasures they had *not* experienced. All that was to come of life was theirs. At that un-tried source of promised happiness they slaked their thirst, and the first eager draught made them drunk with love and joy.

1. Hazlitt, *Complete Works,* ed. P. P. Howe (London: J. M. Dent, 1930–34), 4:248–51.

They were in full possession of their senses and their affections. Their hopes were of air, their desires of fire. Youth is the season of love, because the heart is then first melted in tenderness from the touch of novelty, and kindled to rapture, for it knows no end of its enjoyments or its wishes. Desire has no limit but itself. Passion, the love and expectation of pleasure, is infinite, extravagant, inexhaustible, till experience comes to check and kill it.[2]

Hazlitt then contrasts Shakespeare and "nature" with the "modern philosophy, which reduces the whole theory of the mind to habitual impressions, and leaves the natural impulses of passion and imagination out of the account. . . ." With this he turns to the "Ode":

It is the inadequacy of the same false system of philosophy to account for the strength of our earliest attachments, which has led Mr. Wordsworth to indulge in the mystical visions of Platonism in his Ode on the Progress of Life. He has very admirably described the vividness of our impressions in youth and childhood, and how "they fade by degrees into the light of common day," and he ascribes the change to the supposition of a pre-existent state, as if our early thoughts were nearer heaven, reflections of former trails of glory, shadows of our past being. This is idle. It is not from the knowledge of the past that the first impressions of things derive their gloss and splendour, but from our ignorance of the future, which fills the void to come with the warmth of our desires, with our gayest hopes, and brightest fancies. It is the obscurity spread before it that colours the prospect of life with hope, as it is the cloud which reflects the rainbow. There is no occasion to resort to any mystical union and transmission of feeling through different states of being to account for the romantic enthusiasm of youth; nor to plant the root of hope in the grave, nor to derive it from the skies. Its root is in the heart of man: it lifts its head above the stars. Desire and imagination are inmates of the human breast. The heaven "that lies about us in our infancy" is only a new world, of which we know nothing but what we wish it to be, and believe all that we wish. In

2. Ibid.

youth and boyhood, the world we live in is the world of desire, and of fancy: it is experience that brings us down to the world of reality. What is it that in youth sheds a dewy light round the evening star? That makes the daisy look so bright? That perfumes the hyacinth? That embalms the first kiss of love? It is the delight of novelty, and the seeing no end to the pleasure that we fondly believe is still in store for us. The heart revels in the luxury of its own thoughts, and is unable to sustain the weight of hope and love that presses upon it.—The effects of the passion of love alone might have dissipated Mr. Wordsworth's theory, if he means any thing more by it than an ingenious and poetical allegory. *That* at least is not a link in the chain let down from other worlds: "the purple light of love" is not a dim reflection of the smiles of celestial bliss. It does not appear till the middle of life, and then seems like "another morn risen on mid-day." In this respect the soul comes into the world "in utter nakedness." Love waits for the ripening of the youthful blood. The sense of pleasure precedes the love of pleasure, but with the sense of pleasure, as soon as it is felt, come thronging infinite desires and hopes of pleasure, and love is mature as soon as born. It withers and it dies almost as soon![3]

Hazlitt, like other contemporary writers about passion-love (e.g., Goethe, Shelley, Keats, Stendhal, Schlegel, Constant), does not necessarily predict that it will issue in happiness; indeed, they would say that it usually ends in unhappiness or death. This knowledge, however, does not imply to them that passion-love, like Johnson's "dangerous prevalence of the imagination," ought ideally to be subdued or chastened; rather, since it accords with human nature and since that nature seems more and more to be the target of a variety of modern repressive forces (cf. Hazlitt's "the police spoils all"), it deserves recognition and possible cultivation. Hazlitt's late friend Stendhal pursued *L'amour passion* in *De l'Amour* (1821) to the point that he envisioned its integration not in tragedy but in the comedy of ongoing modern life. He indeed imagined the diminution of the tragic or pathetic conse-

3. Ibid.

quences of passion-love as a function of the emancipation of women into the world both of enlightened education (cf. Mary Wollstonecraft) and of the work force. It is not laying on Wordsworth too heavy a burden of our own programs for social enlightenment to say that, by situating his thoughts about the "Ode" in a study of a play about passion-love, Hazlitt gives the poem a protofeminist critique.

"Juliet," in the course of the play, says Hazlitt, "has become a great girl, a young woman since we first remember her a little thing in the idle prattle of the nurse." That is, she has become an adolescent in this play, as Hazlitt says, of the "progress of life" — an adolescent for whom desire has consequences in failure or success with the beloved companion; desire becomes a social experience.

Similarly, beauty is embodied in the object of desire and found in the experience of desire. In the bourgeois love story, desire produces tragedy because of its social consequences; it cannot participate in social reality but exists beyond it; poetic beauty also must stand over and against historical reality. Hazlitt recognizes the contradiction of beauty without desire. As Herbert Marcuse says: "Beauty is fundamentally shameless,"[4] and as Stendhal says: beauty is "une promesse de bonheur." For Nietzsche beauty awakens "aphrodisiac bliss," just the opposite of the Kantian, Wordsworthian, and Coleridgian wish for a disinterested beauty. When Hazlitt links Wordsworth's doctrine of preexistence to Plato, he is not saying that the poet is Platonic, but that Wordsworth has imported a classicism that no longer applies to the modern world. The happiness of the ancients, segregated to the class of philosophers, now appears in the "Ode" as a regression to an identification with the childlike, that is, to the inconsequential, to a realm free from action and consequences. The attack on Wordsworth's doctrine of preexistence, both from the right (Coleridge) and from the left (Hazlitt), rests ultimately on the confusion of religious salvation and bourgeois leisure envisioned through art. Coleridge labors the inconsistency of the metaphor

4. Herbert Marcuse, *Negations* (Boston: Beacon Press, 1968), 115.

of the child as a philosopher and a prophet: by what route can an innocent gain the knowledge or wisdom imputed to an authority in visionary and intellectual perspective? does not human experience insist on its place in the making of a philosopher? For Hazlitt the raising of hope comes not from a mystical origin before life but from a passional one during life. Both find Wordsworth's epithets for the child confusing and arbitrary. Wordsworth's late explanation that preexistence served as a metaphor is thus enlightening since (*a*) it shifts the focus from the truth of the doctrine to its beauty and, having done so, (*b*) it excuses the confusion and contradiction on artistic grounds (a ploy familiar to New Criticism and some of its more recent descendants).

The second generation of Romantics—Keats, Shelley, Byron, as well as the older Hazlitt—sought to shift the essential human drama from the innocent child and his adoring parents to the adolescent (enmeshed in fantasies of sexual desire and social idealism) and his establishment parents and parent-leaders. (This, of course, is precisely the subject of Blake's prophetic poetry of the 1790s.) One thinks of Keats's young Apollo, of Byron's Don Juan, Shelley's Prometheus and his Alastor-poet—the latter being most directly responsive to the "Ode." What one fears losing is not a visionary gleam that vanishes simply, eternally, or biologically with growing up but the passion of youth, itself a natural biological and psychological phenomenon, but one that inevitably comes into conflict with repressive parental and, by extension, social forces. Wordsworth's own "Romeo and Juliet" was the relationship with Annette Vallon that became the Vaudracour and Julia episode of *The Prelude.* Vaudracour, or "Heartsworth," as David Erdman has translated it, represents the individual as one whose value or worth is in his heart or passions of love. This figure thus defined runs into the conflicts of society from which he retreats into solitude with an "imbecile mind." Such "disappointment" leads to a poem about a loss which art-as-consolation can reverse.

My biggest discovery was that the adolescents studying Wordsworth with me found so compelling Hazlitt's criticism that the

"Ode" has substituted childhood (as idyll) for its real subject, adolescence. I think that my students found the child of the "Ode" empty of action and substance because finally they could, with Hazlitt as advocate, withdraw from the regressed identification with the child as the container of happiness and recover their own more libidinal and aggressive adolescent selves.

Part Seven
Adolescence and
Critical Consciousness

17   The Provocation of
Hazlitt's Intervention

Particularly moving was the ambivalence of my students to Hazlitt's critique of Wordsworth's "Ode," an ambivalence which, as I understand it, can be explained partly in terms of adolescent experience. On the one hand, they found his portrait of Wordsworth in terms of exclusions and his analysis of the poem as an exclusion of passion and adolescent fantasy very compelling, worthy, indeed, of admiration and assent. On the other hand, they found it a terrible intrusion upon the poem, a violation — with all of the traditional moral and sexual implications of that word — a "pollution" of its integrity and purity. The poem, and the institutional encounter with poems, dovetail startlingly with the adolescent rescue fantasy, the wish that the world (for them, the poem) would provide the integrity, firmness, and safety that they themselves tremble to lose or never find. Hazlitt seems, uncannily, to have guessed — in his critique of Wordsworth — what the poet removed from the earlier versions of the poem; that is, he must have recognized that the poem implied the suppression or rationalization of fantasy and desire and not simply its passive omission. For I suspect that the power radiating from the poem to the students includes a system of relief from destabilizing fantasies. It is relevant to consider the "Ode" itself as an answer to some contemporary (late eighteenth-century) portraits of adolescents (or postadolescents) whose desires, fantasies, and

167

ideals led to imprisonment, abandonment, death: Goethe's Werther, Blake's Orc (revolutionary desire), Wordsworth's own Marmaduke (the desolate figure in *The Borderers*), and many others. Even "The Mad Monk" is the monologue of an adolescent whose libidinal and aggressive fantasies have led first to his acting them out and then to his isolation and mental distraction. The "Ode" addresses neither this stage of life nor its implications. But curiously, the *speaking voice* in the poem fits part of the adolescent paradigm:[1] one could describe its progress as radical shifts of mood and perception. It asks global questions about identity: what have I lost? where has it gone and why? who am I? what, finally, have I gained? And it moves back and forth rapidly from discovering meaning in the environment to discovering it in internal states. Yet even more curious, as I have previously observed, is that the adolescent who is present is not acknowledged. The early versions of the poem, with their definitions of the sensual and passional nature of human beings, come much closer to such an acknowledgment. For adolescents part of the comfort granted them by the poem potentially lies in the presence of an adolescent voice, with which they can identify, minus the serious implications of adolescent destabilization, which its acknowledgment would foreshadow.

Before they recognized, however, that the voice of the poem bears resemblance to that of an adolescent, the students, by and large, tried to defend the poem against Hazlitt's onslaughts. What right does he have to insist that the poem be about adolescence? A poet is sincere; he may write about whatever he wishes. Generalizing, any poem is "true," just because the poet says what he says; it is true because it exists and poets write in good faith. Does this, I asked, apply to all writing or just to poems? Primarily poems, they replied, demonstrating again and again how

1. Let me observe that the "speaking voice" in the "Ode" resonates to *any* "season" of one's life in which the perception and risk of change, the turbulence accompanying a re-forming identity, dominate experience. Wordsworth himself, of course, at the time he was writing the "Ode," had entered mid-life, a period of profound self-revaluation.

deeply ingrained in our modern civilization is the granting of
sacrosanct status to the poem. Hazlitt was attacking the poem
as one manifestation of a college student's rescue fantasy. (Interestingly, this view of the poem and the poet is not solely a function of academic literature classes: a student poet in the group
spoke not only of his own but of his poetry teacher's conviction
in the perversity of Hazlitt's truth-seeking criticism.)

It is important, by the way, to make clear that the normal kind
of classroom analysis, the New Critical study of images, patterns,
rhetoric, in general the search for the poem's "meaning" in its
own terms, did not threaten or challenge the students at all. That
approach is essentially a version of the classificatory activity of
Enlightenment thinking: control the object by casting light in
all its dark, secret corners; remove the otherness from the poem.
It is only a step from such a taming of the object to investing
it with the power one wishes: that it rescue one from one's own
inner turbulence.

I have witnessed in this course an example of a student who
revealed in her notebook that the "Ode" gave her permission to
examine and accept the instabilities of her emerging vocational
and social-sexual identities. This occurred only after she and many
other students had gone past the resistance to Hazlitt and had
come to respect his view that Wordsworth had excluded adolescence from the "Ode." Now they could ask the question that simultaneously exercised their critical faculties and led them to
tighten their embrace of the poem's subtextual adolescent vision.
To ask: Where is adolescence in this poem about growing up?
is to ask: Where in the poem, am I? The realization that Hazlitt's provocative questioning was not arbitrary or whimsical but
focused on the mystification of a critical moment in the emergence of identity (a moment that frightened them but also drew
them to it) allowed them freedom to integrate, however tenu-
ously and fragmentarily, some of their fantasy life with their social and intellectual life in school.

How can we further explain the power of Hazlitt's intervention in their romance with the "Ode"? He had, I believe, the ambivalent but awesome status of a parent, but one who identifies

himself in a way that our own subtly repressive society rarely tolerates. Max Horkheimer wrote about the modern attenuation of classic family dynamics in "The End of Reason" (1941):

> In monopolistic society, childhood and adolescence have become mere biological processes. Puberty is no longer a human crisis, for the child is grown up as soon as he can walk, and the grown-up in principle always remains the same. Development has ceased to exist. During the heyday of the family the father represented the authority of society to the child, and puberty was the inevitable conflict between these two. Today, however, the child stands face to face with society at once, and the conflict is decided even before it arises. The world is so possessed by the power of what is and the efforts of adjustment to it, that the adolescent's rebellion, which once fought the father because his practices contradicted his own ideology, can no longer crop up. . . . The process which hardens men by breaking down their individuality—a process consciously and planfully undertaken in the various camps of fascism—takes place tacitly and mechanically in them everywhere under mass culture, and at such an early age that when children come to consciousness everything is settled.[2]

Similarly, the psychiatrist Henry P. Coppolillo writes about the adolescent's inundation with the requirements to elevate "performance as judged by the external world to a position above the concerns for internal integration and comfortable organization that are demanded by the process of development. It is as if we are saying to our youth that while it is permissible to be labeled adolescents, they must not behave as though they were."[3] Both writers refer to the peculiar influence of modern life upon adolescence, to truncate and attenuate it, to deny the kinds of relatively free encounter with parental or other authority that permits the fullness of fantasies of desire and aggression to be

2. Horkheimer, "The End of Reason," in *The Essential Frankfurt School Reader,* ed. Andrew Arato and Eike Gebhardt (New York: Urizen Books, 1978), 41.

3. Henry Coppolillo, "Integration, Organization, and Regulation in Late Adolescence," in *Late Adolescence: Psychoanalytic Studies,* ed. David Dean Brockman (New York: International Universities Press, 1984), 150.

known and integrated into social life. It is as if society understands that the acknowledgment of the fantasy life is a risk to
that society. To the far Right, almost any kind of literature perceived as stimulating imaginative and critical thinking is disrup-
tive to the parent-child relationship, but that relationship is defined with such authoritarianism that it denies the fantasy life
altogether. Hazlitt becomes the parent who allows the fantasy
life of the student to flourish without producing either punishment or anarchy. Hazlitt would be the devil incarnate of "secular humanism," as the far Right labels all proponents of intellectual and emotional independence: the child's "conscience can be
slowly remolded until ultimately he recognizes no need for God
and parental values."[4] Art *may* become the place, in other words,
where an adolescent can truly be an adolescent, where — in Coppolillo's scheme — the adolescent is permitted to extend his drives
and desires toward a beckoning environment, where both the
world and the inner life engage in the making of what have been
called "possible worlds."[5]

For some young people the vital energizing of fantasies into
creative and critical thinking will develop independently of the
kind of strenuous and ascetic exercise I prescribed for my students. But in my experience, for many if not most of them, art — no
matter what its potentially energizing capacity — has already been
sacralized out of the arena of the fantasy life and reified beyond
the life of the mind. They need a Hazlitt who can from time
to time advise them of the import of their own activity. Some
may have felt that Hazlitt had co-opted the play of fantasy with
which they reached towards the "adolescent" voice of the poem
with their own adolescent hunger. Hazlitt, perhaps, took off some
of the magic (or, in Wordsworth's phrase, "colouring of the imagination" or in Benjamin's word, "aura") still on the poem. Some
felt intruded upon. Indeed, I said that the immersion in the his-

4. Barbara Parker and Stephanie Weiss, *Protecting the Freedom to Learn* (Wash-
ington, D.C.: People for the American Way, 1983), 70.
5. See Marvin Lazerson et al., "Learning and Citizenship: Aspirations for
American Education," *Daedalus* 113 (1984): 66.

torical ether of the poem entails a risk to one's initially intense assent to the poet's singing. We risk losing what we think of as freedom. But Hazlitt's evaluative criticism, concerned not with the classification of parts but with truth tested on the pulses of one's knowledge and experience, does not enslave or negate. Freedom in the presence of a work of art, after all, is not (idyllically) constant but fluctuating. Through consciousness we from time to time can still regain the original sensation, but more important, we can develop the freedom of critical consciousness.

"Every ode," wrote one student, "has to define its hero in order to celebrate it." A simple observation, yet this never remained simple when talking about Wordsworth's "Ode." Another student wrote a (rather angry) paper cataloging the emptiness, blindness, passivity of Wordsworth's child: this couldn't be the hero since he is not, in any familiar sense, heroic. Still another student said (as I have already reported) that Wordsworth in the "Ode" exhibits a different, "more disquieting" passion than he expected because "the child isn't real, the heavenly aura isn't real, and the intimations aren't real, but the emotional content of the poem is. . . . Life and death become inconsequential, much in the manner of 'To the Cuckoo' where the earth is 'an unsubstantial, faery place. . . .' The Ode is almost surreal, or dreamlike." For him all that remains in the poem are emotions and fantasies and thoughts. Yet these are the "image" of the adolescent. This, I suspect, is another reason why Hazlitt at once troubled and exhilarated my students: he may have broken (though not finally *damaged*) the magic spell of their adolescent fantasizing, but he also brought them into the consciousness of their own dignity as adolescents through the naming of the real though unacknowledged hero of the poem.

18   The Limits of Beauty
A Traditional Reading of the "Ode"

Toward the end of the course a young woman, in conference, declared that before encountering Wordsworth's "Ode" in history, a poem always seemed to her "like the moon seen on a dark night." This simile, uttered spontaneously as she tried to measure the distance she had traveled, prompted me to ask what image would describe her present experience of poetry; she had no such image. I tentatively took this as confirmation of Allen Grossman's notion that poetry is not an object but should be "the *occasion* for the greatness of persons." As I understand her exquisite self-analysis, she was describing the essence of the traditional bourgeois experience in the presence of the beautiful art object: it dazzles without warmth, defines or reveals itself amidst and because of a surrounding darkness; that is, it exerts its effect by excluding and being excluded by reality, which it does not illuminate. It does not stimulate the mind to act in the world except, perhaps, to reject the world as impure amidst the purity of art. It does, in the darkness, allow for the fullness of the fantasy life but only in its own presence. "What counts as utopia, phantasy, and rebellion in the world of fact is allowed in art. . . . The medium of beauty decontaminates truth and sets it apart from the present. What occurs in art occurs with no obligation. When this beautiful world is not completely represented as something long past . . , it is deprived of concrete relevance by the magic of beauty." My student was beginning to view this as a limited experience, or more precisely an experience with a strict limit placed upon it. If, as Stendhal said, beauty is "une promesse de bonheur," then an encounter with it at some level would demand that the mind of the beholder carry beauty freely into social life. But beauty, in the bourgeois understanding of it, "may be enjoyed in good conscience only in well-delimited areas, with the awareness that it is only for a short period of relaxation or dissipation."[1]

"The moon-symbol," according to Thomas Mann in his essay on Schoepenhauer, "the cosmic parable of all mediation, is art's own. To the old world, to primitive humanity, the planet was strange and sacred in its double meaning, in its median and mediating position in between the solar and the earthly, the spiritual and the material world."[2] Androgynous, femininely receptive and masculinely begetting, the moon stimulates the dialectic of mind, at once receptive and critical, longing for a world of pure spirit yet hungering to engage necessity. But the moon-symbol invoked longingly but critically by my student had lost its fundamental ambiguity; it had become solely the symbol of our willed thrall to the beauty of art. It does not address our restlessness before art, and thus she wished to modify her former experience of beauty as essential to a humanistic education.

Humanism ought to be, in Trilling's phrase, "an enterprise of consciousness," but is it, particularly in today's hypertechnological era? He advocates (in "Why We Read Jane Austen") a study of the arts of the past as fostering an act of empathy which includes a willed imprecision toward the historical reality of the artifact, in turn leading to a greater affirmation of life and of the self as an integer; life and history affirm their worth to us in the deathlike permanence of art. Referring to Keats's "Ode on a Grecian Urn," Trilling finds that the aesthetic and historical modes of perception are assimilated to one another, so that "pastness" is one of the "attributes" of the urn, which is to say that

1. Marcuse, *Negations* (Boston: Beacon Press, 1968), 114–15.
2. Thomas Mann, *Essays of Three Decades*, trans. H. T. Lowe-Porter (New York: Alfred A. Knopf, 1968), 376.

history becomes art, and mind willingly loses its grip on history. Ought this to be an acceptable occasion for an enterprise in consciousness? Does not art, in this sense, exhibit mind in its freedom from necessity? A student wrote in his notebook: "When one experiences a beautiful, positive, extraordinary event, it's hard to believe he is in the realm of reality." Perhaps in ideal circumstances this kind of observation leads to critical reflections on reality, but in my experience of teaching, people associate art (particularly as classroom experience) more with an escape rather than a freedom from necessity, indeed with an escape from thinking rather than with thinking in freedom. Schiller's beautiful formulation of *play* as the fullest expression of the human being as a civilized being, of art as ornament, too often seems to lead to a belief in the self, as revealed through poetry and other forms of art, also as ornament, spinning out its freedom like a top.[3]

There is at work in literary study a necessary economy of mind: if you shine the light of literary analysis very hard upon the object in its internal relations, you have less mind available for work on other matters. The image, as the classical and medieval epic poets have described, is seductive; if Achilles' embrace of the image of Patroclus is a futile gesture, the latter's embrace of the former — that is, the image's hold on the living hero — is nearly overwhelming; Virgil and Dante, even more than Homer, explore this truth. Dante, in order to remain alive on his cosmic journey, must learn to evaluate and judge — not only to love, pity, despise, reject, and "analyze" — the images he engages. Inevitably he must see them as ideas, not held disinterestedly but intently. For us this is comparable to the tentative construction of living contexts for the object, both the context in which the object lived and that in which the reader lives, as if he were Robin-

3. One student, reflecting a year later on the experience of studying the "Ode" for a semester, defined "freedom of mind" this way: "At times I hated the poem for having read it so much. . . . I became so confused. I thought I knew what it was about, but the more I read it the more confusing it became. At the end, however, I seemed to get clearer about the poem but in a different way than in the beginning. What I got out of my confusion was the curiosity to discover the truth."

son Crusoe slowly awakening to his place on a new island: not only the island but himself in relation to it must be known in time. "Poems are occasions of the greatness of persons." A mind must be in the freedom of its thinking occasioned by the poem.

Typically the student in the classroom learns to chain his or her mind to the poem. The poem contains all the answers one might ask of it and provides the language with which to talk about it. Just as someone in the dark shining a light upon an unknown object cannot be seen behind the light, so the student remains invisible (to others but even more to himself) behind the analytic light cast from him onto the poem.

A recent study of the "Ode" by Helen Vendler (see p. 42, n. 3) casts a light so intense upon Wordsworth's poem that it seems no cranny remains in the shadow of mystery or doubt. What she sees is that the poem, in its last three sections, "cures" itself of its disease or "wounds" of despair and loss. It is an instance of self-therapy. Moreover, the "Ode" follows the classical proportions of elegy, moving from despair and loss to their transcendence. Finally, the poet "repossesses" the world through the power of metaphor; that is, the poem is about poetry itself. Not only, in her reading, is there not in the "Ode" a false note struck, but the poem fully and economically "succeeds" in completing its elegiac and therapeutic tasks. The delicate and pervasive images and image patterns prove, by embodying, the poem's curative formulae. Q.E.D. The questions of context, of changing ideas, of conflicting (she would say supporting) early drafts, the responses of Hazlitt, dwindle in significance before this airtight "illumination." It is not that what she says is wrong; it is that she has followed Wordsworth so closely. This critic has not criticized but has analyzed. *What* Wordsworth says, its value and its ideas, are not to be questioned or challenged. Take, for example, her observation that: "Wordsworth is following, in his ode, the classic proportions of elegy. Every elegy descends to that point of death which is reached by Wordsworth in the weight of custom." Of course, Wordsworth is writing with reference to elegy. But the critic needs to observe that, unlike the traditional elegy, no one has died. When Wordsworth writes about a real death it sounds different, e.g.,

"Peele Castle," "Surprised by Joy." The gap between the "proportions" of elegy and the absence of death needs remarking. Similarly the end of the poem "cures" the beginning only in a manner of speaking. (Even Vendler uses inverted commas.) The Mad
Monk needs a cure since he is mad. Freud says we are all neu-
rotic, but Wordsworth imputes choice, not disease, to his speaker:
the whole meditation is a choice made in health.

Yet the category of disease and cure may be congenial to the
experience of the speaker and probably is to Wordsworth, writing in the eighteenth-century poetic tradition of Collins and Mark
Akenside (to say nothing of the tradition of Rousseau), the latter
particularly responsible for associating poetry and the health of
idyllic recoveries from modern isolation and fragmentation. But
Akenside works within a contemporary hypothesis that modern
life creates diseased individuals; it is not a truth or a fact about
human life in modern times. Trilling, criticizing earlier critics
of the "Ode" who said that it signals the departure of Wordsworth's poetic powers, remarked that those critics held "certain
extraneous and unexpressed assumptions . . . about the nature
of the mind."[4] I would say the same for Vendler.

More important for the present task, my students have been
trained to swallow without question Vendler's propositions both
about the "Ode" and about literature generally (e.g., the "Ode"
is about metaphor and poetry itself, and literature is a cure or,
in their associations, a salvation). Students, as well as critics, need
to test their own thinking, their own commitments, as they read.
This is what the community that gathers around literature is for.

There was a time, speaking autobiographically once more,
when Vendler's reading and her analytic way of preceding (and
she stands for an entire tradition of readers) seemed to me apparelled in celestial light. But now — to use Trilling's word for
Wordsworth himself in the conclusion to the "Ode" — I am "ambivalent."[5] I, too, as I have previously shown, respond to the power

4. Bruner, *On Knowing* (Cambridge: Harvard University Press, 1962), 77.
5. That a study of Wordsworth in context should lead to an assessment
of him as "ambivalent" about his propositions suggests that we have moved

of this idyll of self-exploration and recovery and to the brilliant language that carries it; but the questions I have raised with my students do not go away for me. Nor, to be frank, do I think that Wordsworth is entirely honest about his experience and about what he wishes us to know of it. This does not make me feel victorious or arrogant, but neither does it lead to a feeling of emptiness in the presence of Wordsworth.

---

far from the commonly held view that this poet became more conservative and cautious in his thirties and forties than he had previously been. It is rather the tradition of reading him, from Victorian times to the present, along with our cultural predispositions, that has fixed him in a monochromatic conservatism.

19   Beauty, Disappointment, and Sympathy

> Son, I must tell you that madmen intend to
> destroy this beautifully made planet. That
> the murder of our children by these men
> has got to become a terror and a sorrow
> to you, and starting now, it had better in-
> terfere with any daily pleasure.
>
> Grace Paley, "Anxiety"

One student, while being introduced to Wordsworth's "Ode," was, in another class, being introduced to the genocide of the Jews in World War II. Shocked by and riveted to the latter, he wrote in his notebook: "In light of the Holocaust, the language and images of the 'Ode' are quaint." Response to the beautiful requires sensitivity which, as Bertrand Russell (in *Education and the Good Life*) says, primarily manifests itself as sympathy. The world and minds that produced the Holocaust were, of course, supremely deficient in sympathy, and it is our legacy to struggle with the persistence of beauty amidst the persistence of this flourishing moral ugliness. (With the same harrowing consciousness of our contemporary reality another student questioned, upon reading Wordsworth's *Preface*, whether "pleasure" really was the "grand elementary principle.") Yes, in this light, the language of the "Ode" is "quaint," but — I asked this student — does that mean that our curiosity and exploration of its quaintness need to be quaint? The activation of our sympathy in the presence of past and present holocausts has become the greatest challenge of the student of the beautiful, and here the student and his teacher must join hands with contemporary poets like Paul Celan or Nelly Sachs. One sees the challenge taken up in Czeslaw Milosz' "A Song on the End of the World":

179

On the day the world ends
A bee circles a clover,
A fisherman mends a glimmering net.
Happy porpoises jump in the sea,
By the rainspout young sparrows are playing
And the snake is gold-skinned as it should always be.

or in a more recent poem called "Wind" by the British poet of
Cambodian miseries, James Fenton:

This is the wind, the wind in a field of corn.
Great crowds are fleeing from a major disaster
Down the long valleys, the green swaying wadis,
Down through the beautiful catastrophe of wind.

or in Denise Levertov's "The May Mornings":

we remember, ah,
yes, the May mornings,
how could we have forgotten,
what solace it would have been
to think of them,
what solace
it would be in the bitter violence
of fire then ice again we
apprehend — but
it seems the May mornings
are a presence known
only as they pass
lightstepped, seriously smiling, bearing
each a leaflined basket
of wakening flowers.

How often does the teaching of literature, in practice if not
in theory, shut the door against such vital confrontations of
(Wordsworthian) idyllic beauty with the deadly terrors! But all
who labor with art today must try to keep that door open. Beauty
without reference to the terrors produces consolation and satis-

faction; with them it can enspirit an amatory engagement with mental freedom and its consequences in the world.

Empathy, says Trilling, is exercised by humanistic study. Sympathy grows in part from a deeper historical curiosity. Hazlitt exhibited sympathy when he speculated on the biographical source ("disappointment") for Wordsworth's peculiar strength in narrowness and exclusion. The students lingered over his speculation in the midst of their mixed irritation and admiration for Hazlitt's irritation and admiration of their poet. What, biographically, could have brought Hazlitt to such a position? Why was he so engaged? Why so committed to this poet, taken with his strengths but obsessed to define and highlight — again and again — his weaknesses? This led to a reading of Hazlitt's autobiographical essay, "My First Acquaintance with Poets," which calls forth his own disappointment with Coleridge and Wordsworth based on his own late-adolescent idealization of them at age twenty (1798). Suddenly Hazlitt became real and movingly tied to Wordsworth by disappointment in the hope of radical political vision. The difference is that Hazlitt kept the disappointment alive as an instrument of consciousness and his own kind of radical politics. Hazlitt, in essays like "On Going a Journey" or "The Letter-Bell," never abandoned his love of idyllic beauty and the knowledge of its meaning for the imagination's freedom which Wordsworth bequeathed to his Age, but he insisted upon contextualizing it historically amidst a society in which the radical imagination is systematically brutalized. A new level of sympathy for Hazlitt grew as admiration for his strength and independence emerged. But even more important, the nexus between Wordsworth and Hazlitt grows tighter. The "Ode" itself becomes the occasion — in a sense far more immediate to the student enmeshed in the consoling institution of academic literary studies than the numbingly current constructions of Paul Celan — to engage the problem of beauty and consciousness at the end of the twentieth century.

Epilogue

Most of the seminal modern thinkers on education—Whitehead, Dewey, Russell, and more recently Jerome Bruner—all stress, to one degree or another, the interconnectedness of process or method with content. "Education," Bruner said in *On Knowing* (1962), "is a process that cannot, I think, be separated from what it is that one seeks to teach." Most contemporary schemes for high school and college instruction seem to stress one or the other and seem to ask the question: Are we going to teach the students how to think and how to acquire knowledge, or are we going to teach them certain kinds of knowledge? Asked thus, the question cannot possibly lead to a satisfactory answer. Surely the best education does both, although one course may emphasize a method while another the quantity and choice of knowledge. Bruner's understanding of method and content is that they ideally reflect and determine each other. I have tried to follow his advice as thoroughly as I could. One would, I suppose, have to categorize this course just described as a course in method rather than one in content. I was trying to initiate the students into a way of thinking about literature. Moreover, I assumed that they came fully equipped with a method (unacknowledged) and a perspective for reading and writing, a method and a perspective that I attempted to get them to challenge.

On the other hand, while advocating many principles naturally tending toward concern with methodology, I think that the reassessment of the actual matter presented, the content, is at least as important. Ordinarily, in an introductory course in literature, one reads a great range of poems, plays, and one or more novels. They form a collection of autonomous objects to be examined. My students also read many literary artifacts but not as objects historically unrelated to each other. The category of relatedness was historical, not aesthetic. Yet I am sure that art was nonetheless served well, in, for example, the study of genre and the study of imagery. Both came to life out of the necessity for understanding Wordsworth's revisions which, in turn, appeared under the pressures of *zeitgeist* in the form of reviews and literary models. I presented not only content as written artifact but content as intellectual history. The course really was an attempt to present an issue at the heart of the Romantic period and in the history of the received opinion about Romanticism, literary works, and their manipulation in the present society.

Finally, I tried to address the interrelationship between the students' own writing and thinking and that of the "great poet" under scrutiny. Here, perhaps, Bruner's conviction about the interconnectedness of process and content was most critical. How could I best convince students to think powerfully, about things that matter to them and to society, in the presence of literature? Revision, both of their and Wordsworth's work, gave me the means by allowing me to prove, in time, that every stage of writing locks the writer into a particular commitment communicated to an audience and, conversely, no stage of writing can be counted as invisible or self-negating before an inevitable teleology of the artifact. The class became the literary public sitting in judgment before a student's draft. We talked not so much of "improvement" but of "change"; form and content were, by and large, the single object of criticism and review because at issue was the substance, the truth of the argument. We tried to recover the comparable society for Wordsworth and his "Ode." In both instances we assumed that at every step of writing the writer took responsibility for his thinking. The question I gave them to answer on their final paper placed them directly in the path of Hazlitt and de-

manded that they answer *him:* "Can one best describe Wordsworth's 'Ode' by what it excludes?"

Ultimately, as Hazlitt's preoccupation with Wordsworth shows,
this question activates a political consciousness which, according to most analyses of the social personality, reaches into the
realm of drives and fantasies as they shape the way one asks and
answers questions. To bring literature into the realm of politics;
to bring fantasy and reflection into the realm of effective action;
to bring adolescence into its unique exercise of power in the presence of the beautiful, which I hope the years will not diminish,
are the goals of this experiment in education.

Bibliographic Essay

Index

Bibliographic Essay

The following essay gives a short selection of those writings in education, psychology, critical theory, and literary history that have influenced me consciously in this experiment in literary education and that I, in some instances, very much admire.

No study of problems in modern education can afford to neglect Rousseau's 1762 classic, *Emile, or on Education*, trans. Allan Bloom (New York: Basic Books, 1979). To me this has the status of a sacred text, to be at once revered and quarreled with, but above all *known*. Rousseau is the great theorist about the erotic underpinnings of education. To be read in conjunction with *Emile* are its immediate revisionist descendants: (1) Mary Wollstonecraft's *A Vindication of the Rights of Woman*, ed. Carol H. Poston (New York: W. W. Norton, 1975), showing the limits of *Emile* in terms of sexual politics; and (2) Wordsworth's *The Prelude* (1850), modifying Rousseau's idyllic education by stressing the connection between literary experience and human development.

Of the many beautiful modern classics of education, I have responded most to humanist studies such as Alfred North Whitehead's *The Aims of Education* (New York: Macmillan, 1929); John Dewey's *Democracy and Education* (New York: Macmillan, 1916); Bertrand Russell's *Education and the Good Life* (New York: Horace Liveright, 1926); and more recently the writings of Jerome Bruner, especially *Toward a Theory of Instruction* (Cambridge, Mass.: Belknap Press, 1966); and radical studies such as Paul Goodman's *Compulsory Mis-education and the Community of Scholars* (New York: Vintage Books, 1964); Paolo Freire's *Pedagogy of the*

Oppressed (1984) and *Education for Critical Consciousness* (New York: Continuum, 1973); Harold Entwistle's *Antonio Gramsci: Conservative Schooling for Radical Politics* (London: Routledge & Kegan Paul, 1979); and Siegfried Bernfeld's psychoanalytically oriented 1926 essay *Sisyphus, or The Limits of Education,* trans. Frederic Lilge (Berkeley: University of California Press, 1973).

When speaking about "adolescence," I am referring mostly to the writings of Erik Erikson, some of whose eloquent papers are recently collected in *Life History and the Historical Moment* (New York: W. W. Norton, 1975). Erikson's psychohistorical vision is particularly applicable to literary studies. His contemporary, the psychoanalyst Peter Blos observed the adolescent "rescue fantasy," discussed in *On Adolescence: A Psychoanalytic Interpretation* (Glencoe, Ill.: The Free Press, 1962). I found helpful a study in political socialization by M. Kent Jennings and Richard G. Niemi, *The Political Character of Adolescence* (Princeton: Princeton University Press, 1974). Once again, I must refer the reader to *Emile,* which states and reflects the deeply ambivalent attitudes of the Revolutionary period toward the social implications of the adolescent's psychosexual explorations.

The many debates, manifestos, and experiments on the nature, function, and intention of literature and criticism in the past quarter- to half-century have unquestionably affected the ideas in this book. Perhaps the simplest and most challenging statement that long ago rallied me toward the direction taken here comes from Lionel Trilling's "The Meaning of a Literary Idea," the last essay in *The Liberal Imagination* (1979). Trilling, writing in the era of T. S. Eliot's influence and the New Critics, disputes their tendency to separate "idea" from "poem" or to speak about a "literary idea" that does not retain the properties of "ordinary" ideas. Speaking to teachers and critics, he says: ". . . to call ourselves the people of the idea is to flatter ourselves. We are rather the people of ideology, which is a very different thing. Ideology is not the product of thought; it is the habit or ritual of showing respect for certain formulas to which, for various reasons having to do with emotional safety, we have very strong ties of whose meaning and consequences in actuality we have no clear understanding" (p. 277). Anticipating my observations about my students' wish that art be "pure" and suggesting, to me at least, that their wish has ideological roots in Eliot's remark that Henry James had a mind so fine that no *idea* could *violate* it, Trilling says of the New Critics Wellek and Warren that they "seem to think of ideas as masculine and gross and of art as feminine and pure, and . . . permit a union of the two sexes only when ideas give up their masculine, effective nature and 'cease to be ideas in the ordinary sense and become symbols, or even myths.' We naturally ask: symbols of what, myths about what? No anxious exercise of aesthetic theory can make the ideas of, say, Blake and Lawrence other than what they are intended to be—ideas relating to action and to moral judgment" (p. 279).

Trilling, in later years, had difficulty sustaining the implications of this great essay in the presence of the beautiful object, which became more and more for him an object of consolation. The students of this problem who went further in their explorations of modern ambivalence toward the beautiful include Walter Benjamin in his essays on Baudelaire and Kafka and in his famous piece, "The Work of Art in the Age of Mechanical Reproduction," all in *Illuminations,* trans. Harry Zohn (New York: Harcourt, Brace, and World, 1968). The conflict in Benjamin between Marxism and the Jewish mysticism studied profoundly by his friend Gershom Sholem captures in one precise historical dimension a more general problem of cultural criticism and, by extension, of literary education: how to engage and accept the psychosocial fact of response to the beautiful at the same time that one develops a critical consciousness in relation to both the beautiful and one's response to it. No modern study of the beautiful has been more helpful to me than Herbert Marcuse's 1937 essay, "The Affirmative Character of Culture," reprinted in *Negations* (1968), where he sees beauty in capitalist culture as requiring for its affirmation the "bad present" in society but where beauty—as a construct of idealism—also embodies the possibility-in-imagination that something better than what is could be in social reality. Beauty, for Marcuse, also courts and indeed defines the secular soul, that ideological organ transcending, distinguished from, and preferred to the "mind" that can act critically upon reality.

Theodor W. Adorno's "Cultural Criticism and Society," trans. Samuel and Sherry Weber (Cambridge: The MIT Press, 1981) and Louis Althusser's "Ideology and Ideological State Apparatuses" (1971) speak to the person who, inevitably enmeshed in ideology, nonetheless tries to view it critically, "scientifically."

The best recent discussion of the necessity and possibility of accepting the political implications of literary criticism and education in America is Frank Lentricchia's *Criticism and Social Change* (Chicago: University of Chicago Press, 1983). Another fascinating discussion on essentially the same problem is *Against Theory,* ed. W. J. T. Mitchell (Chicago: University of Chicago Press, 1985), a collection of responses to the essay, "Against Theory" by Stephen Knapp and Walter Benn Michaels who claim that "interpretation, the finding of meaning, just *is* the finding of intention" (p. 5) and that in literary studies "true belief and knowledge are the same" (p. 96).

The radical contextualizing of a poem described in this book means a comparably radical contextualizing of the "author" and demands of the student a rethinking of the idea of "author" and "authority," a subject explored in Roland Barthes's "The Death of the Author," in *Image — Music — Text,* trans. Stephen Heath (New York: Hill and Wang, 1977) and Michel Foucault's "What Is an Author?" in *Language, Counter-Memory, Practice,* trans. Donald F. Bouchard and Sherry Simon (Ithaca: Cornell University Press, 1977).

I derived my view of the literary and cultural history of the early post-Enlightenment period from many works, the number and sophistication of which continually increase. Three cultural studies are: Max Horkheimer's and Theodor W. Adorno's 1944 *Dialectic of Enlightenment,* trans. John Cumming (New York: Continuum, 1972), which — though not limited to eighteenth-century versions of "enlightenment" — reveals the power interests behind analytic thinking; Michel Foucault's *Discipline and Punish,* trans. Alan Sheridan (New York: Pantheon Books, 1977), which argues that punishment in the early post-Enlightenment period desisted from forms of bodily torture in order to focus more on the control and manipulation of the live body and mind; and Foucault's *The History of Sexuality, Volume I: An Introduction,* trans. Robert Hurley (New York: Vintage Books, 1980), which carries the preceding argument into the realm of sexuality during the same period, suggesting that sexual and passional expression was perceived by governments and other interested groups as needing not repressive measures but forms of control through the fullness of their visibility and the disarming of their power. This argument bears some relation to that of Horkheimer and Adorno that "enlightenment" thinking was (and still is) a way of controlling "the other" by exposing it "to the light." A fine survey of sexual subjects in European art, music, and literature in the eighteenth century is Jean Hagstrum's *Sex and Sensibility: Ideal and Erotic Love from Milton to Mozart* (Chicago: University of Chicago Press, 1980).

I have tried in the course I taught to disabuse students of the powerful cultural predispositions toward Romantic thinking, which means toward our standard modern ideas about art, creativity, and the response to art, etc. Here are four major books that attempt to revise these predispositions. Raymond Williams' *Culture and Society: 1780–1950* (New York: Columbia University Press, 1958) began by announcing the predicament of the Romantic artist as one forced into an elitism, forced to be a "specialist" in art when the artist in fact often wished to broaden the audience to which he or she was committed. In *The Country and the City* (New York: Oxford University Press, 1973) Williams discussed the vaunted solitude of the Romantic artist, such as Wordsworth, as a culmination in a tradition of eighteenth-century solitaries in which the poetry of rural ease and sweet melancholy was produced in the absence of the recognition of the laboring classes working before the poet's gaze. More recently, Marilyn Butler's *Romantics, Rebels, and Reactionaries: English Literature and Its Background 1760–1830* (New York: Oxford University Press, 1982) brilliantly contextualizes Romanticism by showing that what we ordinarily mean by it belongs probably to one small phase of the historical period. No present-day student can responsibly bypass the work of Butler and of Jerome J. McGann who urges the critical community in America to examine what he calls *The Romantic Ideology* (Chicago: The University of Chicago Press, 1983).

Index

COMPOSED BY METRICOMP, GRUNDY CENTER, IOWA
MANUFACTURED BY EDWARDS BROTHERS, INC.,
ANN ARBOR, MICHIGAN
TEXT AND DISPLAY LINES ARE SET IN BASKERVILLE

Library of Congress Cataloging-in-Publication Data
Robinson, Jeffrey Cane, 1943–
Radical literary education.
Bibliography: pp. 189–193.
Includes index.
1. Wordsworth, William, 1770–1850. Intimations of
immortality.   2. Wordsworth, William, 1770–1850 — Study
and teaching.   3. Odes — History and criticism.
4. Poetry — History and criticism — Theory, etc.
5. Literature — Study and teaching
(Higher) — Case studies.
I. Title.
PR5860.R6   1987   821'.7   86-23366
ISBN 0-299-11060-5
ISBN 0-299-11064-8 (pbk.)